Super Cheap New York Travel Guide

"The skyline of New York is a monument of a splendor that no pyramids or palaces will ever equal or approach." - Ayn Rand.

Titles also by Phil Tang

FREE BOOK: Simply leave an honest review and send a screenshot and proof of purchase to philgtang@gmail.com with the name of the book you'd like free.

COUNTRY GUIDES

Super Cheap AUSTRALIA
Super Cheap AUSTRIA
Super Cheap BAHAMAS
Super Cheap BARBADOS
Super Cheap BERMUDA
Super Cheap BRAZIL
Super Cheap CANADA
Super Cheap DENMARK
Super Cheap FIJI
Super Cheap FINLAND
Super Cheap FRANCE
Super Cheap GRENADA
Super Cheap GERMANY
Super Cheap GREECE
Super Cheap ICELAND
Super Cheap ITALY
Super Cheap IRELAND
Super Cheap JAMAICA
Super Cheap JAPAN
Super Cheap LUXEMBOURG
Super Cheap MALAYSIA
Super Cheap MALDIVES 2024
Super Cheap MEXICO
Super Cheap NETHERLANDS
Super Cheap NEW ZEALAND
Super Cheap NORWAY

Super Cheap SOUTH KOREA
Super Cheap SPAIN
Super Cheap SWITZERLAND
Super Cheap UAE
Super Cheap UNITED KINGDOM
Super Cheap UNITED STATES

CITIES / TOWNS

Super Cheap ADELAIDE 2024
Super Cheap ALASKA 2024
Super Cheap AUSTIN 2024
Super Cheap BANFF 2024
Super Cheap BANGKOK 2024
Super Cheap BARCELONA 2024
Super Cheap BELFAST 2024
Super Cheap BERMUDA 2024
Super Cheap BORA BORA 2024
Super Cheap BRITISH VIRGIN ISLANDS
Super Cheap BUDAPEST 2024
Super Cheap Great Barrier Reef 2024
Super Cheap CAMBRIDGE 2024
Super Cheap CANCUN 2024
Super Cheap CHIANG MAI 2024
Super Cheap CHICAGO 2024
Super Cheap Copenhagen 2024
Super Cheap DOHA 2024
Super Cheap DUBAI 2024
Super Cheap DUBLIN 2024
Super Cheap EDINBURGH 2024
Super Cheap GALWAY 2024
Super Cheap Guadeloupe 2024
Super Cheap HELSINKI 2024
Super Cheap LIMA 2024
Super Cheap LISBON 2024
Super Cheap MALAGA 2024
Super Cheap Martinique 2024
Super Cheap Machu Pichu 2024

Super Cheap MIAMI 2024
Super Cheap Milan 2024
Super Cheap Montpellier 2024
Super Cheap NASHVILLE 2024
Super Cheap NAPA
Super Cheap NEW ORLEANS 2024
Super Cheap NEW YORK 2024
Super Cheap PARIS 2024
Super Cheap PRAGUE 2024
Super Cheap St. Vincent and the Grenadines
Super Cheap SEYCHELLES 2024
Super Cheap SINGAPORE 2024
Super Cheap ST LUCIA 2024
Super Cheap TORONTO 2024
Super Cheap Turks and Caicos 2024
Super Cheap VANCOUVER
Super Cheap VENICE 2024
Super Cheap VIENNA 2024
Super Cheap YOSEMITE 2024
Super Cheap ZURICH 2024
Super Cheap ZANZIBAR 2024

The Magical Power of Bargains

Have you ever felt the rush of getting a bargain? And then found good fortune just keeps following you?

Let me give you an example. In 2009, I graduated into the worst global recession for generations. One unemployed day, I saw a suit I knew I could get a job in. The suit was £250. Money I didn't have. Imagine my shock when the next day I saw the exact same suit (in my size) in the window of a second-hand shop (thrift store) for £18! I bought the suit and after three months of interviewing, without a single call back, within a week of owning that £18 suit, I was hired on a salary far above my expectations. That's the powerful psychological effect of getting an incredible deal. It builds a sense of excitement and happiness that literally creates miracles.

I have no doubt that New York's iconic skyline, bustling streets and rich history will uplift and inspire you, but when you add the bargains from this book to your vacation, not only will you save a ton of money; you are guaranteed to enjoy a truly magical trip to New York.

Who this book is for and why anyone can enjoy budget travel

Did you know you can fly on a private jet for $500? Yes, a fully private jet. Complete with flutes of champagne and re-clinable creamy leather seats. Your average billionaire spends $20,000 on the exact same flight. You can get it for $500 when you book private jet empty leg flights.This is just one of thousands of ways you can travel luxuriously on a budget. You see there is a big difference between being cheap and frugal.

When our brain hears the word "budget" it hears depriva-tion, suffering, agony, even depression. But budget travel need not be synonymous with hostels and pack lunches. You can enjoy an incredible and luxurious trip to New York on a budget, just like you can enjoy a private jet flight for 10% of the normal cost when you know how.

Over 20 years of travel has taught me I could have a 20 cent experience that will stir my soul more than a $100 one. Of course, sometimes the reverse is true, my point is, spending money on travel is the best investment you can make but it doesn't have to be at levels set by hotels and attractions with massive ad spends and influencers who are paid small fortunes to get you to buy into something you could have for a fraction of the cost.

This book is for those who love bargains and want to have the cold hard budget busting facts to hand (which is why we've included so many one page charts, which you can use as a quick reference), but otherwise, the book provides plenty of tips to help you shape your own New York experi-ence.

We have designed these travel guides to give you a unique planning tool to experience an unforgettable trip without spending the ascribed tourist budget.

This guide focuses on New York's unbelievable bargains. Of course, there is little value in traveling to New York and not experiencing everything it has to offer. Where possible, we've included super cheap workarounds or listed the experience in the Loved but Costly section.

When it comes to luxury budget travel, it's all about what you know. You can have all the feels without most of the bills. A few days spent planning can save you thousands. Luckily, we've done the planning for you, so you can distill the information in minutes not days, leaving you to focus on what matters: immersing yourself in the sights, sounds and smells of New York, meeting awesome new people and feeling relaxed and happy.

This book reads like a good friend has travelled the length and breadth of New York and brought you back incredible insider tips.

So, grab a cup of tea or coffee, put your feet up and relax; you're about to enter the world of enjoying New York on the Super Cheap. Oh, and don't forget a biscuit. You need energy to plan a trip of a lifetime on a budget.

Super Cheap New York is <u>not</u> for travellers with the following needs:

1. You require a book with detailed offline travel maps. Super Cheap Insider Guides are best used with Google Maps - download before you travel to make the most of your time and money.

2. You would like thousands of accommodation, food and attraction recommendations; by definition, cheapest is often singular. We only include maximum value recommendations. We purposively leave out over-priced attractions when there is no workaround.

3. You would like detailed write-ups about hotels/Airbnbs/Restaurants. We are bargain hunters first and foremost. We dedicate our time to finding the best deals, not writing flowery language about their interiors. Plus, things change. If I had a pound for every time I'd read a Lonely Planet description only to find the place totally different, I would be a rich man. Always look at online reviews for the latest up-to-date information.

If you want to save A LOT of money while comfortably enjoying an unforgettable trip to New York, minus the marketing, hype, scams and tourist traps read on.

Redefining Super Cheap

The value you get out of Super Cheap New York is not based on what you paid for it; it's based on what you do with it. You can only do great things with it if you believe saving money is worth your time. Charging things to your credit card and thinking 'oh I'll pay it off when I get home' is something you won't be tempted to do if you change your beliefs now. Think about what you associate with the word cheap, because you make your beliefs and your beliefs make you.

I grew up thinking you had to spend more than you could afford to have a good time traveling. Now I've visited 190 countries, I know nothing is further from the truth. Before you embark upon reading our specific tips for New York think about your associations with the word cheap.

Here are the dictionary definitions of cheap:

- Costing very little; relatively low in price; inexpensive: a cheap dress.
- costing little labor or trouble: Words are cheap.
- charging low prices: a very cheap store.
- Of little account; of small value; mean; shoddy: Cheap conduct; cheap workmanship.
- Embarrassed; sheepish: He felt cheap about his mistake.
- Stingy; miserly:
  He's too cheap to buy his own brother a cup of coffee.

Three out of six definitions have extremely negative connotations. The 'super cheap' we're talking about in this book is not shoddy, embarrassed, or stingy.
We added the super to reinforce our message. Super's dictionary definition stands for 'a super quality'. Super Cheap stands for enjoying the best on the lowest budget. Question other people's definitions of cheap so you're not blinded to possibilities, poten-

tial, and prosperity. Here are some new associations to consider forging:

Shoddy

Cheap stuff doesn't last is an adage marketing companies have drilled into consumers. However, by asking vendors the right questions cheap doesn't mean something won't last. I had a $10 backpack last for 8 years and a $100 suitcase bust on the first journey.

A study out of San Francisco University found that people who spent money on experiences rather than things were happier. Memories last forever, not things, even expensive things. And as we will show you during this guide, you don't need to pay to create glorious memories.[1]

Embarrassed

I have friends who routinely pay more to vendors because they think their money is putting food on this person's table. Paradoxically, Cuban doctors are driving taxis because they earn more money; it's not always a good thing for the place you're visiting to pay more and can cause unwanted distortion in their culture - Airbnb pushing out renters is an obvious example. Think carefully about whether the extra money is helping people or incentivising greed.

Stingy

Cheap can be eco-friendly. Buying thrift clothes is cheap, but you also help the Earth. Many travellers are often disillusioned by the reality of traveling since the places on our bucket-lists are overcrowded. Cheap can take you away from the crowds. You can find balance and harmony being cheap. "Remember a journey is

---

[1]   Paulina Pchelin & Ryan T. Howell (2014) The hidden cost of value-seeking: People do not accurately forecast the economic benefits of experiential purchases, The Journal of Positive Psychology, 9:4, 322-334, DOI: 10.1080/17439760.2014.898316

best measured in friends, rather than miles." – Tim Cahill. And making friends is free!

A recent survey by Credit Karma found 50% of Millennials and Gen Z get into debt traveling. **Please don't allow credit card debt to be an unwanted souvenir you take home.** As you will see from this book, there's so much you can enjoy in New York for free, some many unique bargains and so many ways to save money! You just need to want to!

Discover New York

Vibrant, dynamic, and multifaceted, New York is a city that defies simple description. It's magnetic, electric, and diverse—towering skyscrapers, bustling streets, and a melting pot of cultures converge to create an unforgettable urban experience. Yet, even these adjectives fail to capture the essence of New York; it's a place that must be experienced firsthand to be truly understood.

Founded by the Dutch in 1624 as 'New Amsterdam,' the city later fell under British control in 1664 and was renamed New York. Today, the city pulses with life as yellow cab drivers honk their horns, hot dog vendors line street corners, and fashionistas strut the sidewalks in true Sex and the City style. A visit to Times Square feels like stepping onto the set of a quintessential New York movie—a surreal experience that epitomizes the city's larger-than-life allure.

Home to 8.6 million people, including 78 billionaires, New York comprises five boroughs: Manhattan, The Bronx, Queens, Brooklyn, and Staten Island. Despite its affluent residents, the city offers abundant opportunities to explore on a budget. From leisurely strolls through city streets adorned with skyscrapers to free museum visits, public building tours, and picnics in scenic parks, there's no shortage of affordable or no-cost activities. And let's not forget the culinary delights of Chinatown, Little Italy, and Soho, where you can indulge in fabulous yet budget-friendly eats.

As E.B. White once reflected, New York is akin to poetry—it compresses all facets of life into its small island confines, accompanied by the symphony of internal engines and bustling streets.

While it caters to tourists from around the globe, savvy travelers know that the key to an affordable trip lies in venturing off the beaten path and discovering local deals and hidden gems. By following the advice in this guide, visitors can experience the magic of New York without leaving their bank balances in disarray. With careful planning, it's entirely possible to enjoy the city on a budget, with daily expenses—accommodation included—averaging around $60. So, dive into the heart of the Big Apple and let its energy and spirit leave an indelible mark on your soul.

Some of New York's Best Bargains

Kayak for free

Hire a free kayak from the Boathouse at Brooklyn Bridge Park on Wednesdays, Thursdays and Saturdays through summer. https://www.brooklynbridgepark.org/ No experi-

ence is necessary, and volunteers are on hand to provide instruction and guidance as you paddle along the waterfront.

Go for Gold

Ever wondered where New York City keeps its gold re-
serves? Take a free tour of the Federal Reserve Bank of
New York and get a behind-the-scenes look at its famous
gold vault, which houses billions of dollars worth of gold
bars.

Watch a Baseball game on the cheap

Baseball is any self-respecting New Yorkers passion. 162 Baseball games are played between April and October. Whether you choose to support The New York Yankees or The New York Mets you can score tickets for a paltry $15! You can book cheap tickets here: https://gametime.co/new-york-yankees-tickets

If basketball is more your thing head to The West 4th Street Basketball Courts in Greenwich Village, known informally as "The Cage". This is where scouts go to find the next Micheal Jordan.

Enjoy Free events and activities

On about any day of the year, you can find something fun, informative, healthy and FREE to enjoy in a New York park. NYC Parks is the ultimate source of free outdoor events. See whats on during your visit https://www.nycgovparks.org/events

Time Out NYC also maintain a list of free events happening around the city: https://www.timeout.com/newyork/things-to-do/free-things-to-do-today For up to date freebies, check out NYC for FREE.

Daily Deal Websites

The city is teeming with opportunities to save money on attractions, dining, entertainment, and more. When it comes to finding the best deals and discounts for attractions, dining, and entertainment in NYC, there are several websites that can help you save money while exploring the city. Here are some of the top ones:

- **Groupon:** Groupon offers deals on a wide range of activities, restaurants, and experiences in NYC. From sightseeing tours to spa treatments and dining vouchers, Groupon often has discounted offers that can help you save on your adventures in the city.
- **LivingSocial:** Similar to Groupon, LivingSocial provides deals and discounts on various attractions, dining experiences, and events in NYC. It's worth checking regularly for discounted offers on activities and experiences that interest you.
- **Time Out New York:** Time Out New York is a comprehensive resource for finding events, restaurants, bars, and attractions in NYC. They often feature special promotions, discounts, and deals for readers, making it a valuable tool for saving money while exploring the city.
- **The Official NYCgo Website:** NYCgo is the official tourism website for New York City, offering information on attractions, events, dining, and more. They frequently feature special offers and discounts for tourists, so be sure to check their website for deals before planning your itinerary.
- **Goldstar:** Goldstar specializes in offering discounted tickets for theater, concerts, sporting events, and other live entertainment in NYC. It's a great place to find last-minute deals on Broadway shows, comedy clubs, and other performances.

- **StubHub:** While StubHub is best known for selling tickets to sports events and concerts, they also offer discounted tickets to Broadway shows, comedy performances, and other entertainment options in NYC. Keep an eye out for deals and promotions on their website.
- **Restaurant.com:** For dining deals in NYC, Restaurant.com offers discounted gift certificates to a variety of restaurants in the city. You can often find deals where you can purchase a $25 gift certificate for as little as $10.

Do a free tour of Grand Central

The Municipal Arts Society of New York conduct daily free 75minute tours of Grand Central Station at 12.30pm (the meeting point is the information booth on the Grand Concourse). For more information visit www.mas.org

Dine on delicious Korean

Danji serves the best bulgogi beef sliders in New York. You can get a lunch menu for a mere $13, dinner menu from $23 and a tasting menu, with all of the best options on the menu for $55. Address: 346 W 52nd Street

Take advantage of Fleet Week

During the last-week of May; when sailors invade New York you can take free tours of ships arriving from all across the globe.

Do a free tour of Liberty Island

Park Rangers lead free tours on the island home to the Statue of Liberty. Tours are 40 minutes. The tours chronicle the islands history during 1892 and 1924; the busiest years of immigration.

Do a free tour of New York Distilling Company

Brooklyn Brewery offers free tours, weekends between noon and 6pm. For an up-to-date schedule visit www.brooklyn-brewery.com.

Like your libations? Here are the Best Happy Hours in New York:

- 169 Bar.
- Bonnie Vee.
- Fresh Salt.
- Huertas.
- Mister Paradise.
- The Mermaid Inn.
- Alfie's Kitchen & Craft Beer Bar.
- Fools Gold NYC.

Visit during restaurant week

If you're a foodie, visit during NYC Restaurant Week. A biannual event that has been held every summer and winter since 1992. Back then, only a few restaurants took part in the promotion, while this year's event has over 500 participating restaurants . Over time, the length of Restaurant Week has been extended so that we can now enjoy almost a full month of great, affordable food instead of just a week. Many of New York's top chefs - Jean-Georges Vongerichten, Daniel Boulud, Marcus Samuelsson and Leah Cohen cook during the week. There are 3 price options at NYC Restaurant Weeks 2023: $30 (for lunch), $45 (for dinner) and $60 (for both). they're spread across all five boroughs (with the majority being in Manhattan). The the Winter one takes place from mid-January to mid-February, and the Summer one from mid-July to mid-August. Reserve your tables in advance: https://www.nycgo.com/restaurant-week

Discount Passes

In NYC, membership cards like the New York Pass, City-PASS, and Explorer Pass can offer substantial savings, providing access to many attractions for one price. Each option has its benefits, depending on your interests and length of stay, so it's worth comparing to see which offers the best savings for your visit.

New York Pass - Access to over 100 attractions - Higher upfront cost Starting from $134 (1 day)
- Skip-the-line privileges - Limited validity period (1-10 days)
- Savings on bundled admissions - Must visit multiple attractions to maximize value

CityPass - Bundled admissions to top attractions - Limited selection of attractions Starting from $132 (9 days)
- Skip-the-line privileges - Must use within a specified time frame
- Validity period of up to 9 days - Limited customization options

NYC Explorer Pass - Customizable attraction selection - Limited skip-the-line privileges Starting from $64 (2 choices)
- Savings of up to 50% off regular admission prices - Must choose attractions carefully to maximize value
- Valid for up to 30 days - Not suitable for travelers with limited time or specific attraction preferences

How to Enjoy ALLOCATING Money in New York

'Money's greatest intrinsic value—and this can't be overstated—is its ability to give you control over your time.' - Morgan Housel

Notice I have titled the chapter how to enjoy allocating money in New York. I'll use saving and allocating interchangeably in the book, but since most people associate saving to feel like a turtleneck, that's too tight, I've chosen to use wealth language. Rich people don't save. They allocate. What's the difference? Saving can feel like something you don't want or wish to do and allocating has your personal will attached to it.

And on that note, it would be helpful if you considered removing the following words and phrase from your vocabulary for planning and enjoying your New York trip:

- Wish

- Want

- Maybe someday

These words are part of poverty language. Language is a dominant source of creation. Use it to your advantage. You don't have to wish, want or say maybe someday to New York. You can enjoy the same things millionaires enjoy in New York without the huge spend.

'People don't like to be sold-but they love to buy.' - Jeffrey Gitomer.

Every good salesperson who understands the quote above places obstacles in the way of their clients' buying. Companies create waiting lists, restaurants pay people to queue outside in order to create demand. People reason if something is so in demand, it must be worth having but that's often just marketing. Take this sales maxim 'People don't like to be sold-but they love to buy and flip it on its head to allocate your money in New York on things YOU desire. You love to spend and hate to be sold. That means when something comes your way, it's not 'I can't afford it,' it's 'I don't want it' or maybe 'I don't want it right now'.

Saving money doesn't mean never buying a latte, never taking a taxi, never taking vacations (of course, you bought this book). Only you get to decide on how you spend and on what. Not an advice columnist who thinks you can buy a house if you never eat avocado toast again.

I love what Kate Northrup says about affording something: "If you really wanted it you would figure out a way to get it. If it were that VALUABLE to you, you would make it happen."

I believe if you master the art of allocating money to bargains, it can feel even better than spending it! Bold claim, I know. But here's the truth: Money gives you freedom and options. The more you keep in your account and or invested the more freedom and options you'll have. The principal reason you should save and allocate money is TO BE FREE! Remember, a trip's main purpose is relaxation, rest and enjoyment, aka to feel free.

When you talk to most people about saving money on vacation. They grimace. How awful they proclaim not to go wild on your vacation. If you can't get into a ton of debt enjoying your once-in-a-lifetime vacation, when can you?

When you spend money 'theres's a sudden rush of dopamine which vanishes once the transaction is complete. What happens in the brain when you save money? It increases feelings of security and peace. You don't need to stress life's uncertainties. And having a greater sense of peace can actually help you save more money.' Stressed out people make impulsive financial choices, calm people don't.'

The secret to enjoying saving money on vacation is very simple: never save money from a position of lack. Don't think 'I wish I could afford that'. Choose not to be marketed to. Choose not to consume at a price others set. Don't save money from the flawed premise you don't have enough. Don't waste your time living in the box that society has created, which says saving money on vacation means sacrifice. It doesn't.

Traveling to New York can be an expensive endeavor if you don't approach it with a plan, but you have this book which is packed with tips. The biggest other asset is your perspective.

How to feel RICH in New York

You don't need millions in your bank to **feel rich**. Feeling rich feels different to every person.

"Researchers have pooled data on the relationship between money and emotions from more than 1.6 million people across 162 countries and found that **wealthier people feel more positive "self-regard emotions" such as confidence, pride and determination.**"

Here are things to see, do and taste in New York, that will have you overflowing with gratitude for your luxury trip to New York.

- Achieving a Michelin Star rating is the most coveted accolade for restaurants but those that obtain a Michelin Star are synonymous with high cost, but in New York there are restaurants with Michelin-stars offering lunch menus for 30 dollars or less! If you want to taste the finest seasonal local dishes while dining in pure luxury, here are the 8 Most Affordable Michelin Restaurants in New York:

- Casa Enrique I $47 per person.
- Claro I $48 per person.
- Oxomoco I $50 per person.
- Contra I $53 per person.
- Meadowsweet I $55 per person.
- Don Angie I $55 per person.
- The Musket Room I $55 per person.
- Rezdôra I $60 per person.

If fine dining isn't your thing, don't worry further on in the guide you will find a range of delicious cheap eats in New York that deserve a Michelin-Star.

- While money can't buy happiness, it can buy cake and isn't that sort of the same thing? Jokes aside, Fay Da Bakery (83 Mott St) is a Chinese Bakery in New York have turned cakes and pastries into edible art.

- While you might not be staying in a penthouse, you can still enjoy the same views. Visit rooftop bars in New York, like Cantina Rooftop to enjoy incredible sunset views for the price of just one drink. And if you want to continue enjoying libations, head over to 169 Bar for a dirt-cheap happy hour, lots of reasonably priced (and delicious) cocktails and cheap delicious snacks.

- Walking out of a salon or barber shop with a fresh cut makes most people feel rich. As the maxim goes, if you look good, you feel good. If you crave that freshly blow-dried or trimmed look, become a hair model salonmodel.co in New York. You'll receive a completely free cut/colour or wash. Of course, always agree on the look with your stylist.

Those are just some ideas for you to know that visiting New York on a budget doesn't have to feel like sacrifice or constriction. Now let's get into the nuts and bolts of New York on the super cheap.

Planning your trip

When to visit

The first step in saving money on your New York trip is timing. If you are not tied to school holidays, the best time to visit is during the shoulder-season months April to June and September to early November when the weather is warmer but the tourist crowds are fewer. The cheapest time to visit New York is on weekends from mid-January to the end of February but winter weather can be extreme.
In the summer take advantage of rooftop movies, and concerts on the beach at Coney Island and free yoga in Bryant Park. Don't despair if you are visiting during peak times there are innumerable hacks to save on accommodation in New York which we will go into detail on.

When you visit will determine the luxury level of your accommodation. If staying in a five-star hotel is a must for you in NYC, then arrange your visit for the low season or shoulder months.

AVOID The weekend price hike in peak season

Hostel and hotel prices skyrocket during weekends in peak season. If you can get out of New York for the weekend if you visit in the peak season you'll save $$$ on your accommodation. For example a dorm room at a popular Hostel costs $44 a night during the week. That price goes to $253 for Saturday's and Sundays.

Visit New York on your birthday

Companies know rewarding customers on their birthdays will boost retention so many in New York go out of their way to surprise customers and make them feel special on their birthdays.

Visit New York on your birthday you can get well over $250 of free stuff, meals, cakes and more. All you need is a valid ID to claim your birthday gifts.

Here are the free gifts:

- Free beauty gift from Sephora ($15)
- Free beauty gift from Ulta rewards
- Go to Build-a-Bear on a child's birthday and you pay your age for the bear! Great way to save $20 if you're travelling with kids.

And here's where you can sample a free meal, birthday treat or heavy discount:

- Capital Grille – get free dessert with your meal!
- Baskin Robbins – a free scoop!
- Sprinkles Cupcakes – a free birthday cupcake!
- Panera – a free pastry!
- Starbucks Coffee - show your loyalty card and get a free coffee
- Jamba Juice - free juice.
- List of New York Birthday Freebies
- Anthony's Coal Fired Pizza - a FREE 12" Pizza.
- IKEA - FREE restaurant meal + $15 store gift certificate.
- Krispy Kreme free dozen donuts.

Here is a regularly updated list of NYC Birthday freebies: https://www.favoritecandle.com/free-birthday-meals/New-York/NY

What's on month by month in NYC

Here's a breakdown of events and activities month by month:

January:

- New Year's Eve Celebration in Times Square
- Winter Restaurant Week
- Winter Jam in Central Park (weather permitting)
- Broadway Week (2-for-1 tickets)

February:

- Lunar New Year Parade in Chinatown
- Valentine's Day events and specials
- New York Fashion Week
- The Westminster Kennel Club Dog Show

March:

- St. Patrick's Day Parade
- Macy's Flower Show
- NYC Half Marathon
- Tribeca Film Festival (usually towards the end of the month)

April:

- Cherry Blossom Festival at Brooklyn Botanic Garden
- The Orchid Show at the New York Botanical Garden
- Tartan Day Parade
- Tribeca Film Festival continues

May:

- Fleet Week

- Memorial Day Weekend events and parades
- NYC Vegetarian Food Festival
- Governors Ball Music Festival

June:

- Pride Month events, including the Pride Parade
- Shakespeare in the Park begins
- Museum Mile Festival
- SummerStage concerts begin

July:

- Macy's Fourth of July Fireworks
- Summer Restaurant Week
- Harlem Week
- New York Musical Festival (NYMF)

August:

- U.S. Open Tennis Championships
- Lincoln Center Out of Doors Festival
- Hong Kong Dragon Boat Festival
- West Indian American Day Carnival & Parade

September:

- New York Fashion Week
- Labor Day Weekend events
- San Gennaro Feast in Little Italy
- Feast of San Gennaro

October:

- New York Comic Con
- Oktoberfest events
- Open House New York
- Halloween Parade in Greenwich Village

November:

- New York City Marathon
- Macy's Thanksgiving Day Parade

- New York Comedy Festival
- Holiday markets begin to open

December:

- Rockefeller Center Christmas Tree Lighting
- Holiday window displays on Fifth Avenue
- Hanukkah and Christmas celebrations
- New Year's Eve celebrations in Times Square

Free festivals in NYC

Festival Name	Date	Location
Shakespeare in the Park	June - August	Delacorte Theater, Central Park
Harlem Week	August	Various locations in Harlem
Governors Island Art Fair	September	Governors Island
West Indian American Day Parade	Labor Day	Eastern Parkway, Brooklyn
Bryant Park Film Festival	Summer	Bryant Park
SummerStage	June - September	Various parks throughout NYC
Coney Island Mermaid Parade	June	Coney Island
Jazz Age Lawn Party	June & August	Governors Island
Dance Parade	May	Tompkins Square Park
Washington Square Outdoor Art Exhibit	May & September	Washington Square Park
New York International Fringe Festival	August	Various locations

Where to stay?

This is a personal preference and should be based on your interests and what attractions you plan to visit in the city. Midtown East (near Grand Central Terminal) is good for exploring the city. The best price/ performance ratio is East Williamsburg.

Long Island City is good if you want great **views of the Manhattan skyline** – just not too far to the east of Long Island, places like Montauk and the Hamptons are not budget.

Areas to avoid
DO NOT STAY OUTSIDE of the city. You will be reliant on the train schedule and round-trip tickets to Grand Central were $25 per person during peak hours ($20 off-peak). When traveling with a group, the price of train tickets can add up and you will be better off using that money towards a room in the city.

The cheapest place to stay
If you're travelling solo hostels are your best option in New York, both for meeting people and saving pennies. Well-reviewed   is conveniently located in East Williamsburg and they offer dorms from $20. We stayed in an Airbnb as we were two so it was cheaper - and we took the transit bus in to the city. Airbnbs are expensive in New York but work out cheaper if you are travelling as a group.

Local Discount Accommodation

Aside from Booking and Airbnb you can find discount b and b's on this site: https://www.cozycozy.com/us/manhattan-bed-and-breakfast

Money Mistakes

Mistake	Solution
Taking taxis every-where in NYC	Use public transportation like the subway or buses, or walk when possible. Consider rideshare services or apps like Uber or Lyft for longer distances.
Eating at tourist trap res-taurants	Research and explore local eateries, food markets, and food trucks for more authentic and budget-friendly options. Read reviews online or ask locals for recommendations.
Paying full price for at-tractions	Look for discounted tickets online, through hotel con-cierge services, or consider purchasing attraction passes like the New York Pass or CityPASS for bundled savings.
Over-looking free or low-cost activities	Take advantage of free attractions such as Central Park, museums with suggested donations, street per-formances, walking tours, and exploring neighbor-hoods on foot. Check for free events and festivals happening during your visit.
Not budget-ing for tips	Remember to budget for tips, especially in restaur-ants, bars, taxis, and for services like luggage hand-ling or tour guides. Follow standard tipping practices in the U.S., typically 15-20% of the total bill.

Ignoring currency ex-change rates	Avoid exchanging money at airports or tourist areas where rates may be less favorable. Use ATMs to withdraw local currency or use credit cards with no foreign transaction fees for purchases.
Falling for scams or overpay-ing for souven-irs	Be cautious of scams targeting tourists, such as fake ticket sellers, unauthorized tour guides, or street vendors selling counterfeit goods. Research prices for souvenirs and negotiate when appropriate.

NYC Minus the crowds

During peak tourist seasons such as summer and the holiday season (Thanksgiving through New Year's), popular attractions, landmarks, and areas like Times Square and Central Park can indeed feel very crowded due to the influx of the 60 million tourists who visit each year. Here are some recommendations for enjoying top attractions in NYC while avoiding crowds:

Visit Early in the Day or Late in the Evening:
Many attractions are less crowded during the early morning or late evening hours. Consider visiting popular sites such as Times Square, Central Park, or the Empire State Building during these times to experience them with fewer people around.
Weekdays Over Weekends:
Weekdays generally have fewer tourists compared to weekends. Plan your visits to major attractions like museums, landmarks, and shopping areas on weekdays to avoid large crowds.
Off-Peak Seasons:
Take advantage of visiting NYC during off-peak seasons, such as January through March (excluding holidays), or late September through November. During these times, hotels may offer lower rates, and attractions are typically less crowded.
Book Timed Entry Tickets in Advance:
For popular attractions like the Statue of Liberty, One World Observatory, or the 9/11 Memorial Museum, consider purchasing timed entry tickets online in advance. This allows you to bypass long lines and ensures a more streamlined experience.
Explore Neighborhoods Outside of Manhattan:
Venture beyond the tourist-heavy areas of Manhattan and explore neighborhoods in the other boroughs such as Brooklyn, Queens, or the Bronx. You'll find unique cultural experiences, local eateries, and attractions with fewer crowds.

Utilize Early Bird or Late Night Specials:

Some attractions offer early bird or late-night specials with discounted admission prices during non-peak hours. Check attraction websites or inquire with ticket vendors for any special offers available.

Take Guided Tours During Off-Peak Times:

If you prefer guided tours, opt for tours during off-peak times when group sizes are smaller. You'll have a more intimate experience and better interaction with the guide without large crowds.

Plan Outdoor Activities on Weekdays:

If you're planning outdoor activities like biking in Central Park or walking across the Brooklyn Bridge, aim for weekdays when foot traffic is lighter compared to weekends.

Consider Alternate Attractions:

Instead of visiting the most famous landmarks, consider exploring lesser-known attractions or hidden gems in NYC. You'll still experience the city's charm without the crowds.

Monitor Crowd Levels with Apps and Websites:

Use crowd-tracking apps or websites to monitor the busiest times at popular attractions. This information can help you plan your visits accordingly to avoid peak hours.

Hack your New York Accommodation

Your two biggest expenses when travelling to New York are accommodation and food. This section is intended to help you cut these costs dramatically before and while you are in New York.

Hostels are the cheapest accommodation in New York but there are some creative workarounds to upgrade your stay on the cheap.

Use Time

There are two ways to use time. One is to book in advance. Three months will net you the best deal, especially if your visit coincides with an event. The other is to book on the day of your stay. This is a risky move, but if executed well, you can lay your head in a five-star hotel for a 2-star fee.

Before you travel to New York, checked for big events using a simple google search 'What's on in New York', if you find no big events drawing travellers, risk showing up with no accommodation booked (If there are big events on demand exceeds supply and you should avoid using this strategy). Start checking for discount rooms at 11 am using a private browser on booking.com.

Before I go into demand-based pricing, take a moment to think about your risk tolerance. By risk, I am not talking about personal safety. No amount of financial savings is worth risking that. What I am talking about is being inconvenienced. Do you deal well with last-minute changes? Can you roll with the punches or do you freak out if something changes? Everyone is different and knowing yourself is the best way to plan a great trip. If you are someone that likes to have everything pre-planned using demand-based pricing to get cheap accommodation will not work for you. Skip this section and go to blind-booking.

Demand-based pricing
Be they an Airbnb host or hotel manager; no one wants empty rooms. Most will do anything to make some revenue because they still have the same costs to cover whether the room is occupied or not. That's why you will find many hotels drastically slashing room rates for same-day bookings.

How to book five-star hotels for a two-star price
You will not be able to find these discounts when the demand exceeds the supply. So if you're visiting during the peak season, or during an event which has drawn many travellers again don't try this.

On the day of your stay, visit booking.com (which offers better discounts than Kayak and agoda.com). Hotel Tonight individually checks for any last-minute bookings, but they take a big chunk of the action, so the better deals come from booking.com. The best results come from booking between 2 pm and 4 pm when the risk of losing any revenue with no occupancy is most pronounced, so algorithms supporting hotels slash prices. This is when you can find rates that are not within the "lowest publicly visible" rate. To avoid losing customers to other websites, or cheapening the image of their hotel most will only offer the super cheap rates during a two hour window from 2 pm to 4 pm. Two guests will pay 10x difference in price but it's absolutely vital to the hotel that neither knows it.

Takeaway: To get the lowest price book on the day of stay between 2 pm and 4 pm and extend your search radius to include further afield hotels with good transport connections.

Where to stay if you want to walk to major attractions

If you want to stay in a central location where you can easily walk to major attractions in New York City, Manhattan is your best bet. Manhattan is home to many iconic landmarks, museums, theaters, and shopping districts, making it an ideal base for exploring the city on foot. Here are some neighborhoods in Manhattan where you can stay and walk to major attractions:

- **Midtown Manhattan:** Midtown is one of the most bustling and tourist-friendly areas in NYC, known for its skyscrapers, Broadway theaters, and iconic landmarks like Times Square, Rockefeller Center, and the Empire State Building. Staying in Midtown puts you within walking distance of many major attractions, as well as excellent dining and shopping options.
- **Chelsea:** Chelsea is a vibrant neighborhood in Manhattan known for its art galleries, High Line park, and trendy dining scene. Staying in Chelsea provides easy access to attractions like the High Line, Chelsea Market, and the Whitney Museum of American Art.
- **Greenwich Village:** Greenwich Village is a charming and historic neighborhood in downtown Manhattan, known for its tree-lined streets, historic buildings, and bohemian vibe. Staying in Greenwich Village puts you within walking distance of attractions like Washington Square Park, NYU, and the West Village.

- **Lower Manhattan (Financial District/Tribeca):** Lower Manhattan is home to many historic landmarks, including the Statue of Liberty, One World Trade Center, and Wall Street. Staying in this area allows you to explore attractions like the 9/11 Memorial & Museum, Battery Park, and the Oculus transportation hub.
- **Upper West Side:** The Upper West Side is a residential neighborhood known for its beautiful brownstones, Central Park, and cultural institutions like the American Museum of Natural History and Lincoln Center. Staying on the Upper West Side provides easy access to Central Park and the Museum Mile along Fifth Avenue.
- **Upper East Side:** The Upper East Side is another residential neighborhood with upscale shops, restaurants, and cultural institutions like the Metropolitan Museum of Art and the Guggenheim Museum. Staying on the Upper East Side allows you to explore Museum Mile and Central Park's eastern side.

Priceline Hack to get a Luxury Hotel on the Cheap

Priceline.com has been around since 1997 and is an incredible site for sourcing luxury Hotels on the cheap in New York. If you've tried everything else and that's failed, priceline will deliver.

Priceline have a database of the lowest price a hotel will accept for a particular time and date. That amount changes depending on two factors:

1. Demand: More demand high prices.
2. Likelihood of lost revenue: if the room is still available at 3pm the same-day prices will plummet.

Obviously they don't want you to know the lowest price as they make more commission the higher the price you pay.

They offer two good deals to entice you to book with them in New York. **And the good news is neither require last-minute booking (though the price will decrease the closer to the date you book).**

'Firstly, 'price-breakers'. You blind book from a choice of three highly rated hotels which they name. Pricebreakers, travelers are shown three similar, highly-rated hotels, listed under a single low price.' After you book they reveal the name of the hotel.

Secondly, the 'express deals'. These are the last minute deals. You'll be able to see the name of the hotel before you book.

To find the right luxury hotel for you at a cheap price you should plug in the
neighbourhoods you want to stay in, an acceptable rating (4 or 5 stars), and filter by the amenities you want.

You can also get an addition discount for your New York hotel by booking on their dedicated app.

Hotels with frequent last-minute booking discounts:

Here are several four and five-star hotels in Manhattan that offer comfortable accommodations are centrally located, and frequently have heavy last-minute booking discounts. We have included the regular pricing for comparison:

The Hotel @ Times Square - Offering clean and comfortable rooms, free breakfast, and a convenient location near Times Square, starting from around $120 per night.

Hotel Newton - Featuring spacious and comfortable rooms, free breakfast, and a convenient location near Central Park, starting from around $130 per night.
Holiday Inn Manhattan 6th Ave - Chelsea - Offering modern and well-appointed rooms, a fitness center, and a conve-

nient location in Chelsea, starting from around $140 per night.

The Watson Hotel - Housed in a retro-chic building, this hotel offers spacious rooms, a rooftop pool, and a convenient location near Columbus Circle, starting from around $150 per night.

How to trick travel Algorithms to get the lowest hotel price

Do not believe anyone who says changing your IP address to get cheaper hotels or flights does NOT work. If you don't believe us, download a Tor Network and search for flights and hotels to one destination using your current IP and then the tor network (a tor browser hides your IP address from algorithms. It is commonly used by hackers). You will receive different prices.

The price you see is a decision made by an algorithm that adjusts prices using data points such as past bookings, remaining capacity, average demand and the probability of selling the room or flight later at a higher price. If knows you've searched for the area before ip the prices high. To circumvent this, you can either use a different IP address from a cafe or airport or data from an international sim. I use a sim from Three, which provides free data in many countries around the world. When you search from a new IP address, most of the time, and particularly near booking you will get a lower price. Sometimes if your sim comes from a 'rich' country, say the UK or USA, you will see higher rates as the algorithm has learnt people from these countries pay more. The solution is to book from a local wifi connection - but a different one from the one you originally searched from.

Super cheap and Un-usual places to stay in New York City

Here are some unique options with starting prices to consider:

1. **Capsule Hotels:** Capsule hotels offer minimalist accommodations with small, pod-like sleeping quarters. While not common in NYC, you may find options like Pod 39 or Pod Times Square with starting prices around $50 to $80 per night for a single pod.
2. **Hostels:** Hostels provide budget-friendly accommodations and a communal atmosphere. Look for hostels like HI NYC Hostel or The Local NYC with starting prices ranging from $30 to $50 per night for a dorm bed.
3. **Boatels:** Boatels are boat hotels docked in marinas around NYC, offering a nautical experience with stunning skyline views. Prices vary depending on the boat size and amenities, but you may find options starting around $100 to $150 per night for a private cabin.
4. **Camping in NYC Parks:** Some NYC parks offer camping options during certain times of the year, providing a budget-friendly way to experience the outdoors in the city. Prices can vary, but you may find options starting around $30 to $50 per night for a tent site.

• **Floyd Bennett Field:** Located in Brooklyn within the Gateway National Recreation Area, Floyd Bennett Field offers camping options during certain times of the year. Campgrounds are available for tents and RVs, providing a unique outdoor experience within the city limits.

- **Jamaica Bay Wildlife Refuge:** Also part of the Gateway National Recreation Area in Brooklyn and Queens, Jamaica Bay Wildlife Refuge may offer limited camping opportunities during special events or organized programs. However, camping availability is generally limited, and it's advisable to check with park authorities for details.
- **Pelham Bay Park:** Located in the Bronx, Pelham Bay Park is the largest park in New York City and offers a range of recreational activities. While camping options within the park itself are limited, nearby Orchard Beach RV Park provides camping facilities for RVs and trailers.
- **Croton Point Park:** Located just north of NYC in Croton-on-Hudson, Croton Point Park offers camping facilities with tent and RV sites. The park is situated along the Hudson River and provides scenic views of the surrounding landscape.
- **Harriman State Park:** While not within the city limits, Harriman State Park is located within an hour's drive of NYC and offers extensive camping options. With over 200 campsites, the park provides opportunities for tent camping, RV camping, and cabin rentals in a natural setting.

The Airbnb Ban

The Airbnb ban in New York City ban banned stays of fewer than 30 consecutive days. This ban aims to regulate the growing short-term rental market, which has been blamed for exacerbating issues such as housing affordability, neighborhood disruptions, and illegal hotel operations.

1. **Entire Home Rentals:** The ban primarily targets entire home rentals where the host is not present during the guest's stay. This means that renting out an entire apartment or house for short-term stays of fewer than 30 days is generally prohibited unless the host is present. Meaning, you can still find a room in a home.
2. **Areas Affected:** The ban on short-term rentals applies citywide to all five boroughs of New York City, including Manhattan, Brooklyn, Queens, the Bronx, and Staten Island. It covers both rent-stabilized and market-rate apartments, as well as properties in designated historic districts and landmarked buildings.
3. **Penalties:** Violating the ban on short-term rentals can result in significant penalties, including fines of up to $7,500 for the first offense and escalating fines for repeat violations. Hosts found to be operating illegal short-term rentals may also face eviction proceedings and other legal consequences.

Nearby Places to stay where Airbnb is allowed

Finding places near New York City where Airbnb is allowed and with affordable commuting options can be challenging due to regulations and varying transportation costs. However, here are some suggestions for areas near NYC with relatively cheaper accommodations and reasonable commuting options:

1. Jersey City, New Jersey:

Jersey City is located just across the Hudson River from Manhattan and offers a range of Airbnb options at relatively lower prices compared to NYC.
Commuting to NYC is convenient via the PATH train, which provides quick access to downtown and midtown Manhattan. Look for accommodations near PATH stations like Journal Square, Grove Street, or Newport.
Additionally, ferries and buses also connect Jersey City to NYC, providing alternative commuting options.

2. Hoboken, New Jersey:

Hoboken is another city located across the Hudson River from Manhattan, known for its vibrant community and waterfront views of NYC.
Airbnb accommodations in Hoboken may be more affordable compared to NYC, especially in neighborhoods near PATH stations like Hoboken Terminal.
Commuting to NYC via the PATH train or ferry from Hoboken is quick and convenient, with easy access to various parts of Manhattan.

3. Weehawken, New Jersey:

Weehawken is a township located along the Hudson River with stunning views of the NYC skyline.
While options may be limited, Airbnb accommodations in Weehawken can offer a quieter alternative to staying in NYC.
Commuting to NYC via ferries or buses is available, providing scenic views of Manhattan during the commute.

The cheapest way to commute from New Jersey to New York City depends on factors such as your starting point in New Jersey, your destination in NYC, and your preferences for travel time and convenience. In general, Path is cheapest:

1. **Public Transportation - PATH Train:**
   - The PATH (Port Authority Trans-Hudson) train connects various cities in New Jersey, including Hoboken, Jersey City, and Newark, to several locations in Manhattan, such as the World Trade Center, Herald Square, and 33rd Street.
   - Fares for the PATH train are relatively inexpensive, typically ranging from $2.75 to $3.00 per ride, depending on the destination. Discounted fares may be available with the use of a SmartLink card or other fare payment methods.
   - The PATH train operates frequently throughout the day, making it a convenient and cost-effective option for commuting between New Jersey and NYC.

How to get last-minute discounts on owner rented properties

In addition to Airbnb, you can also find owner rented rooms and apartments on www.vrbo.com or HomeAway or a host of others.

Nearly all owners renting accommodation will happily give renters a "last-minute" discount to avoid the space sitting empty, not earning a dime.

Go to Airbnb or another platform and put in today's date. Once you've found something you like start the negotiating by asking for a 25% reduction. A sample message to an Airbnb host might read:

Dear HOST NAME,

I love your apartment. It looks perfect for me. Unfortunately, I'm on a very tight budget. I hope you won't be offended, but I wanted to ask if you would be amenable to offering me a 25% discount for tonight, tomorrow and the following day? I see that you aren't booked. I can assure you, I will leave your place exactly the way I found it. I will put bed linen in the washer and ensure everything is clean for the next guest. I would be delighted to bring you a bottle of wine to thank you for any discount that you could offer.

If this sounds okay, please send me a custom offer, and I will book straight away.

YOUR NAME.

In my experience, a polite, genuine message like this, that proposes reciprocity will be successful 80% of the time. Don't ask for more than 25% off, this person still has to pay the bills and will probably say no as your stay will cost them more in bills than they make. Plus starting higher, can offend the owner and do you want to stay somewhere, where you have offended the host?

In Practice

To use either of these methods, you must travel light. Less stuff means greater mobility, everything is faster and you don't have to check-in or store luggage. If you have a lot of luggage, you're going to have fewer of these opportunities to save on accommodation. Plus travelling light benefits the planet - you're buying, consuming, and transporting less stuff.

Blind-booking

If your risk tolerance does not allow for last-minute booking, you can use blind-booking. Many hotels not wanting to cheapen their brand with known low-prices, choose to operate a blind booking policy. This is where you book without knowing the name of the hotel you're going to stay in until you've made the payment. This is also sometimes used as a marketing strategy where the hotel is seeking to recover from past issues. I've stayed in plenty of blind book hotels. As long as you choose 4 or 5 star hotels, you will find them to be clean, comfortable and safe. priceline.com, Hot Rate® Hotels and Top Secret Hotels (operated by lastminute.com) offer the best deals.

Hotels.com Loyalty Program

This is currently the best hotel loyalty program with hotels in New York. The basic premise is you collect 10 nights and get 1 free. hotels.com price match, so if booking.com has a cheaper price you can get hotel.com, to match. If you intend to travel more than ten nights in a year, its a great choice to get the 11th free.

Don't let time use you.

Rigidity will cost you money. You pay the price you're willing to pay, not the amount it requires a hotel to deliver. Therefore if you're in town for a big event, saving money on accommodation is nearly impossible so in such cases book three months ahead.

The best price performance location in New York

A room putting New York attractions, restaurants, and nightlife within walking distance will save you time on transport. However restaurants and bars don't get that much cheaper the further you go from famous tourist attractions. But you will also get a better idea of the day to day life of a local if you stay in a neighbourhood like East Williamsburg. It depends on the New York you want to experience. For the tourist experience stay in the centre either in a last-minute hotel or Airbnb. For a taste of local life the urban cool district of East Williamsburg is the best you will find. Groupon, Roomorama and Living Social. Both offer significant deals on New York City hotels.

What to do if you only find overpriced options

If when you're searching for accommodation, you can only find overpriced offers, it's likely that you're visiting at a time where demand outstrips supply. In this case, have a look at www.trustedhousesitters.com. You stay for free when you care for someones pets. If you really can't find a good deal, this can be worth doing but only you know if you want to make a commitment to care for someone else's pets while on vacation. Some find it relaxing, others don't. The properties in New York can be even more stunning than five-star hotels but if you're new to house sitting you might be against 10+ applicants, so make sure your profile is really strong before you apply for a sit. It could save you a small fortune and, who knows, you could even make some new (furry and non-furry) friends.

Cheapest Hotel Chains in NYC:

- **Pod Hotels:** Pod Hotels offer compact, budget-friendly accommodations in convenient locations across NYC.
- **Super 8 by Wyndham:** While primarily known for budget accommodations, Super 8 has a few locations in NYC with relatively affordable rates.
- **Holiday Inn Express:** Holiday Inn Express properties in NYC often offer reasonable rates for travelers seeking basic amenities and comfort.
- **Best Western:** Best Western has several locations in NYC offering budget-friendly accommodations with standard amenities.
- **Comfort Inn:** Comfort Inn properties in NYC may provide affordable rates for travelers seeking comfort on a budget.

Cheapest Four-Star Hotels in NYC:

Finding truly cheap four-star hotels in NYC can be challenging, but some options may offer relatively lower rates compared to others:

- **Row NYC:** While rates can vary depending on demand, Row NYC, located in Times Square, sometimes offers competitive rates for a four-star property.
- **The Gallivant Times Square:** Another option in the Times Square area, The Gallivant, occasionally offers reasonable rates for a four-star hotel.
- **The Roosevelt Hotel:** Located near Grand Central Terminal, The Roosevelt Hotel may have competitive

rates for a four-star property, particularly during off-peak times.

- **Hotel Pennsylvania:** Situated near Penn Station, Hotel Pennsylvania sometimes offers affordable rates for its four-star status, especially during slower seasons.
- **Hilton Garden Inn Times Square:** While not always the cheapest, Hilton Garden Inn Times Square can occasionally offer competitive rates for a four-star hotel in a prime location.

Universities renting dorm rooms in summer

Some universities rent out dorm rooms during the summer months when students are typically on break. This can provide an affordable accommodation option for travelers. Here are a few universities in NYC known to offer summer dorm rentals:

- **New York University (NYU):** NYU often offers summer housing options in their dormitories located in Greenwich Village and other parts of Manhattan. Prices vary depending on the dormitory and room type.
- **Columbia University:** Columbia University provides summer housing options in their dormitories located in Morningside Heights, Upper Manhattan. They offer accommodations for individuals and groups at varying price points.
- **The New School:** The New School offers summer housing in their dormitories located in Greenwich Village and other areas of Manhattan. They provide both single and shared rooms at different price levels.
- **Fordham University:** Fordham University may offer summer housing options in their dormitories on the Lincoln Center campus or the Rose Hill campus in the Bronx. Prices vary depending on the room type and amenities.

It's recommended to contact the housing offices of these universities directly or visit their websites for more informa-

tion on availability, rates, and booking procedures for summer dorm rentals.

Convent stays

**While prices can vary, staying in a convent or
monastery often involves a donation rather than a fixed
nightly rate. Here are a few options:**

- **St. Joseph's Residence:** Located in the East
  Village, St. Joseph's Residence offers affordable accommodations in a convent setting. Visitors are typically asked to make a donation for their stay.
- **St. Francis Friary:** This Franciscan friary in
  Manhattan may offer accommodations to travelers
  seeking a quiet retreat. Visitors are usually asked to
  make a donation for their stay.
- **Sacred Heart Monastery:** Situated in Harlem,
  Sacred Heart Monastery provides simple accommodations in a peaceful environment. Guests may be
  asked to contribute a donation for their stay.

Sleep pods in NYC

If you need to stay central for a short-time, sleep pods can
work:

- **Pod 39 Hotel:** Located in Midtown Manhattan, Pod
  39 Hotel offers "Pod Bunk" rooms, which are essentially upscale bunk beds with privacy curtains, individual lights, and outlets. While not traditional sleep
  pods, they provide a similar concept of compact and
  affordable accommodations within a shared space.
  Prices for Pod Bunk rooms typically start around
  $100-$150 per night.
- **The Jane Hotel:** Situated in the West Village, The
  Jane Hotel offers "Cabin" rooms, which are small,

ship cabin-inspired accommodations with bunk beds. While not exactly sleep pods, they provide a cozy and budget-friendly option for solo travelers. Prices for Cabin rooms at The Jane Hotel start around $100-$200 per night.

The pro's and con's of each Borough

Let's take a look at the pros and cons of each borough in New York:

Manhattan:
    Pros: Manhattan is the heart of NYC, known for iconic landmarks like Times Square, Central Park, and the Empire State Building. It offers a plethora of world-class restaurants, Broadway shows, museums, and shopping districts like Fifth Avenue. With its efficient public transportation system, tourists can easily navigate the borough. Manhattan also boasts a vibrant nightlife scene with trendy bars and clubs.
    Cons: The cost of accommodations, dining, and entertainment in Manhattan tends to be higher compared to other boroughs. The bustling streets can feel crowded and overwhelming, especially in tourist-heavy areas like Times Square. Safety concerns may arise in certain neighborhoods, particularly late at night.

Brooklyn:
    Pros: Brooklyn offers a diverse mix of cultures, neighborhoods, and attractions. Visitors can explore iconic landmarks like the Brooklyn Bridge and Prospect Park, as well as trendy neighborhoods like Williamsburg and DUMBO. Brooklyn's culinary scene is renowned for its artisanal eateries, food markets, and ethnic restaurants. The borough also hosts cultural events, street festivals, and art galleries.
    Cons: While Brooklyn provides a more affordable alternative to Manhattan, some neighborhoods may still have relatively high costs for accommodations and din-

ing. Safety can vary by neighborhood, with certain areas experiencing higher crime rates. Tourists may find it less convenient to access Manhattan attractions from some parts of Brooklyn.

Queens:
Pros: Queens is the most ethnically diverse borough, offering a rich tapestry of cultures, cuisines, and experiences. Tourists can visit attractions like the Queens Museum, Flushing Meadows-Corona Park, and the Unisphere. The borough is home to vibrant neighborhoods like Astoria, Long Island City, and Jackson Heights, each with its own unique charm. Queens also provides more affordable accommodations compared to Manhattan.
Cons: While Queens offers cultural diversity, it may lack the iconic landmarks and attractions that draw tourists to Manhattan. Some parts of Queens may have limited access to public transportation, making it challenging to navigate without a car. Safety can vary by neighborhood, with certain areas experiencing higher crime rates.

The Bronx:
Pros: The Bronx offers attractions such as the Bronx Zoo, New York Botanical Garden, and Yankee Stadium. Visitors can explore cultural institutions like the Bronx Museum of the Arts and enjoy outdoor activities in parks like Van Cortlandt Park and Pelham Bay Park. The borough provides more affordable accommodations compared to Manhattan, with a range of dining options reflecting its diverse communities.
Cons: The Bronx may have a reputation for higher crime rates in certain neighborhoods, although safety has improved in recent years. While the borough is well-connected by public transportation, travel times to Manhattan attractions can be longer compared to other bor-

oughs. The Bronx may lack the same level of tourist infrastructure and amenities as Manhattan.

Staten Island:

Pros: Staten Island offers a more laid-back and suburban atmosphere compared to the other boroughs. Tourists can enjoy attractions like the Staten Island Ferry, Staten Island Zoo, and Historic Richmond Town. The borough boasts scenic waterfront views, parks, and hiking trails, making it a great destination for outdoor enthusiasts. Accommodations and dining options in Staten Island tend to be more affordable compared to Manhattan.

Cons: Staten Island is the least densely populated borough and may lack the bustling energy and cultural attractions found in Manhattan and Brooklyn. While the Staten Island Ferry provides free transportation to Manhattan, travel times can be longer, and tourists may find limited options for nightlife and entertainment on the island. Safety concerns in certain areas may also affect tourists' experiences.

Each borough is further divided into neighborhoods, districts, or communities. These subdivisions within each borough vary in size, character, and amenities.

Here are a few suburbs outside of NYC with average price ranges for accommodation:

- **Jersey City, New Jersey:** Located just across the Hudson River from Manhattan, Jersey City offers relatively more affordable accommodations compared to NYC. Prices for hotels and Airbnbs in Jersey City can range from $80-$200 per night, depending on the location and type of accommodation.
- **Hoboken, New Jersey:** Another city across the river from Manhattan, Hoboken is known for its lively waterfront area and historic charm. Prices for accom-

modations in Hoboken can range from $100-$300 per night, depending on factors such as proximity to the waterfront and amenities offered.

- **Long Island City, Queens:** Long Island City is a neighborhood in Queens known for its rapidly growing skyline and proximity to Manhattan. Prices for hotels and Airbnbs in Long Island City can range from $100-$300 per night, depending on factors such as location and proximity to public transportation.
- **Astoria, Queens:** Astoria is a diverse neighborhood in Queens known for its cultural attractions and dining scene. Prices for accommodations in Astoria can range from $80-$200 per night, depending on factors such as location and amenities offered.
- **Brooklyn:** Various neighborhoods in Brooklyn offer a range of accommodation options at different price points. Prices for accommodations in Brooklyn can vary widely depending on the neighborhood, with options ranging from budget-friendly to more upscale. Generally, prices for hotels and Airbnbs in Brooklyn can range from $80-$300+ per night.

When searching for accommodations outside of NYC, it's essential to factor in transport costs into the city.

How to be a green tourist in New York

New York like other major cities struggles with high levels of air pollution. The city suffered years of severe smog, with instances like the harming thousands of residents. Thankfully the and local legislation has provided for much needed improvements. Still its important as responsible tourists that we help not hinder New York. There is a bizarre misconception that you have to spend money to travel in an eco-friendly way. This like, all marketing myths was concocted and hyped by companies seeking to make money off of you. In my experience, anything with eco in front of their names e.g Eco-tours will be triple the cost of the regular tour. Don't get me wrong sometimes its best to take these tours if you're visiting endangered areas, but normally such places have extensive legislation that everyone, including the eco and non-eco tour companies must comply with. The vast majority of ways you can travel eco-friendly are free and even save you money:

- Avoid Bottled Water - get a good water bottle and refill. The water in New York is safe to drink.

- Thrift shop but check the labels and don't buy polyester clothes - overtime plastic is released into the ocean when we wash polyester.

- Don't put your shopping in a plastic bag, bring a cotton tote with you when you venture out.

- Pack Light - this is one of the best ways to save money. If you find a 5-star hotel for tonight for $10, and you're at an Airbnb or hostel, you can easily pack and upgrade hassle-free. A light pack equals freedom and it means less to wash.

- Travel around New York on Bikes or e-Scooters or use Public Transportation. Car Pool with services like bla bla car or Uber/Lyft share.

- Walk, this is the best way to get to know New York. You never know what's around the corner.

Saving Money on Food in New York City

Use 'Too Good To Go'

Annually, the city sees about 3.9 million tons of food waste end up in landfills, contributing significantly to methane gas production. Yet, amidst this stark reality, there lies a beacon of hope and innovation. Organizations like Too Good To Go, City Harvest, GrowNYC, and Rethink Food NYC lead the charge in rescuing this precious sustenance and you can use TGTG to save money while eating incredible food and saving carbon!

New York offers plenty of food bargains; if you know where to look. Thankfully the app 'Too Good to Go' is turning visitors into locals by showing them exactly where to find the tastiest deals and simultaneously rescue food that would otherwise be wasted. In New York you can pick up a $15 buy of baked goods, groceries, breakfast, brunch, lunch or dinner boxes for $2.99. You'll find lots of fish and meat dishes on offer in New York, which would normally be expensive.

How it works? You pay for a magic bag (essentially a bag of what the restaurant or bakery has leftover) on the app and simply pick it up from the bakery or restaurant during the time they've selected. You can find extremely cheap breakfast, lunch, dinner and even groceries this way. Simply download the app and press 'my current location' to find the deals near you in New York. What's not to love about delicious food thats a quarter of the normal price and helping to drive down food waste?

Here are some of the best Magic Bags in New York:

Magnolia Bakery: This bakery (made famous by Sex and The City) is famous for its cupcakes and other baked goods. You can get a box of assorted cupcakes for a heavily discounted price.

Whole Foods: Some Whole Foods locations offer a Too Good To Go option for their prepared food section. Y

Fresh&Co: This chain of healthy food restaurants offers a Too Good To Go option for their unsold salads, sandwiches, and bowls.

Osteria Morini: This Italian restaurant offers a Too Good To Go option for their evening menu. You can get a three-course meal for a discounted price.

Bagel Hole: This bagel shop offers a Too Good To Go option for their unsold bagels. You can get a bag of assorted bagels for a super discounted price.

Le Pain Quotidien: This bakery and cafe chain often offers Too Good To Go bags with assorted baked goods, sandwiches, salads, and other items at a discounted price. With multiple locations throughout NYC, it's a convenient option for grabbing a bag of surplus food on the go.

Pret A Manger: Pret A Manger, a popular grab-and-go chain, occasionally offers Too Good To Go bags with surplus sandwiches, salads, snacks, and drinks at discounted prices. It's a convenient option for grabbing a quick and affordable meal in NYC.

Eataly: This Italian marketplace offers Too Good To Go bags with surplus items from its various departments, including fresh pasta, cheeses, meats, bread, and desserts. With locations in Flatiron and Downtown NYC, Eataly's bags offer a taste of Italy at a discounted price.

Dunkin' Donuts: Some Dunkin' Donuts locations in NYC participate in the Too Good To Go program, offering bags with surplus donuts, bagels, muffins, and other baked goods at discounted prices. It's a sweet deal for fans of Dunkin' looking to save money on their favorite treats.

An oft-quoted parable is 'There is no such thing as cheap food. Either you pay at the cash registry or the doctor's office'. This dismisses the fact that good nutrition is a choice; we all make every-time we eat. Cheap eats are not confined to hotdogs and kebabs. The great thing about using Too Good To Go is you can eat nutritious food cheaply: fruits, vegetables, fish and nut dishes are a fraction of their supermarket cost.

Japan has the longest life expectancy in the world. A national study by the Japanese Ministry of Internal Affairs and Communications revealed that between January and May 2019, a household of two spent on average ¥65,994 a month, that's $10 per person per day on food. You truly don't need to spend a lot to eat nutritious food. That's a marketing gimmick hawkers of overpriced muesli bars want you to believe.

Check out this local Facebook group (https://www.facebook.com/groups/471563341060101/) where people share pictures of the food they picked up from restaurants and supermarkets in New York. It's a great way to see what's on offer and find food you'll love.

Our favourite magic bags in New York come from Der Pioneer and Windsor Terrace. Never pick up a bag with a rating lower than 4.2 on the Too Good To Go app. People using it tend to be kinder because its fighting food waster. PLEASE don't waste your time on places with a rating below 4.2.

New York City is a melting pot of cultures, and its food scene reflects this diversity. From street food carts to Michelin-starred restaurants, NYC offers a culinary experience like no other. The city's food culture is shaped by its immigrant communities, historical influences, and a constant influx of new culinary trends. In this essay, we'll explore the popular dishes of New York City, their histories, and strategies for saving money on food, including websites and apps.

Popular Dishes of New York City

- **Pizza:** New York-style pizza is legendary, known for its thin crust, foldable slices, and generous toppings. This iconic dish traces its roots to Italian immigrants who brought their pizza-making skills to NYC in the early 20th century. Some of the most famous pizza joints include Lombardi's Pizza in Little Italy and Di Fara Pizza in Brooklyn.
- **Bagels:** NYC bagels are a breakfast staple, prized for their chewy texture and flavorful crust. Jewish immigrants introduced bagels to NYC in the late 19th century, and they quickly became a beloved local food. Ess-a-Bagel in Midtown and Russ & Daughters on the Lower East Side are renowned for their traditional bagels and lox.
- **Hot Dogs:** Street food vendors have been serving hot dogs in NYC since the late 19th century. A quintessential New York experience is grabbing a hot dog from a cart and topping it with mustard, sauerkraut, or onions. Gray's Papaya and Nathan's Famous are famous hot dog spots in NYC.
- **Pastrami Sandwich:** The pastrami sandwich is a NYC classic, featuring thinly sliced, smoked beef

brisket served on rye bread with mustard. Jewish delis like Katz's Delicatessen in the Lower East Side are famous for their pastrami sandwiches, which have been a NYC tradition for over a century.

- **Cheesecake:** New York-style cheesecake is rich, creamy, and decadent, with a dense texture and graham cracker crust. The origins of cheesecake date back to ancient Greece, but the New York version became popular in the early 20th century. Junior's Restaurant in Brooklyn is renowned for its classic New York cheesecake.
- **Burgers:** NYC boasts a vibrant burger scene, with options ranging from classic diner-style burgers to gourmet creations. The hamburger's history in NYC dates back to the 19th century, and today, burger joints like Shake Shack and The Spotted Pig are beloved by locals and visitors alike.
- **Dollar Slices:** In recent years, dollar slice pizza has become a ubiquitous part of NYC's food landscape. These no-frills pizza joints offer cheap slices of pizza for just a dollar or two, making them popular among budget-conscious New Yorkers and tourists.
- **Ramen:** Ramen shops have proliferated in NYC, offering comforting bowls of Japanese noodles in savory broth. Ramen's popularity in NYC can be traced to the late 20th century, and today, establishments like Ippudo and Momofuku Noodle Bar are known for their delicious ramen offerings.

While dining out in NYC can be expensive, there are several strategies for saving money on food, including using websites and apps to find deals and discounts.

- **Restaurant Reservation Platforms:** Websites and apps like OpenTable and Resy allow you to make reservations at NYC restaurants and often offer special deals, such as discounted prix fixe menus or exclusive promotions.

- **Discount Dining Programs:** Some credit card companies and loyalty programs offer discounts and rewards for dining at participating restaurants in NYC. For example, American Express's "Amex Offers" program often includes dining deals at select establishments.
- **Restaurant Week:** NYC Restaurant Week, held biannually in the summer and winter, offers prix fixe lunch and dinner menus at participating restaurants for a fraction of the regular price. It's a great way to sample dishes from some of NYC's top restaurants at a discounted rate.
- **Happy Hour Specials:** Many bars and restaurants in NYC offer discounted drinks and appetizers during happy hour, typically on weekday afternoons or evenings. Websites like HappyHourFinder.com can help you find happy hour deals in your area.
- **Food Delivery Apps:** Apps like Seamless, Grubhub, and Uber Eats often offer discounts and promotional codes for first-time users or during off-peak hours. Additionally, subscribing to their newsletters or following them on social media can help you stay updated on special offers.
- **BYOB Restaurants:** Bringing your own bottle of wine or beer to a restaurant can help you save money on alcohol, as many establishments charge high markups on drinks. Websites like BYOBGuide.com list BYOB restaurants in NYC.
- **Local Markets and Food Halls:** Visiting local markets and food halls, such as Chelsea Market or Smorgasburg, can be a more budget-friendly alternative to dining out. These venues offer a variety of food options at various price points, allowing you to sample different cuisines without breaking the bank.

Cheapest Champagne Bars:

Champagne bars in NYC tend to have higher prices due to the exclusivity of the drink, but some may offer more budget-friendly options or happy hour specials:

- **Ruffian Wine Bar & Chef's Table:** Located in the East Village, Ruffian offers a curated selection of natural wines, including some sparkling options. While not exclusively a champagne bar, they have a cozy atmosphere and may offer more affordable bubbly choices.
- **Air's Champagne Parlor:** Situated in Greenwich Village, Air's Champagne Parlor offers a wide selection of champagnes and sparkling wines. While prices can vary, they may have more affordable options available by the glass or during happy hour.
- **Corkbuzz Wine Studio:** With locations in Union Square and Chelsea Market, Corkbuzz offers a selection of sparkling wines, including champagne, in a casual and welcoming atmosphere. They often have wine specials and events that may feature affordable champagne options.

Please note that prices for champagne can vary significantly depending on the brand, vintage, and size of the pour, so it's best to check with the establishment for current pricing.

Cheap Michelin-Starred Restaurants:

While Michelin-starred restaurants are typically associated with high prices, there are a few in NYC that offer more affordable options:

- **L'Appart:** Located in Battery Park City, L'Appart is a Michelin-starred restaurant offering French cuisine in an intimate setting. They offer a reasonably priced lunch menu with multiple courses, making it a more budget-friendly option to experience Michelin-starred dining.

- **Casa Enrique:** This Michelin-starred Mexican restaurant in Long Island City, Queens, offers authentic and flavorful dishes at relatively affordable prices. It's a great option for those looking to enjoy high-quality cuisine without breaking the bank.

Cheapest Tasting Menus:

Tasting menus in NYC can vary widely in price, but some restaurants offer more affordable options for those on a budget:

- **Hearth:** Located in the East Village, Hearth offers a seasonal tasting menu featuring farm-to-table American cuisine. While prices may vary depending on the ingredients and number of courses, Hearth generally offers tasting menus at relatively affordable prices compared to other fine dining establishments.
- **Ukiyo:** This Japanese restaurant in Brooklyn offers an omakase tasting menu at a more affordable price point compared to some other sushi restaurants in NYC. While still a special dining experience, Ukiyo's omakase menu may be more accessible to budget-conscious diners.

Hit the oyster happy hours

Love oysters? Go to an Oyster Happy Hour at Jeffery's Grocery, The Dead Rabbit, upstate craft beer & oyster bar, Sel Rrose or Crave Fishbar. Many of the places mentioned offer $2 oysters weekdays from 4 p.m. to 7 p.m.

Don't eat Italian food in Little Venice

Though the food is excellent, the prices are touristy prices. Instead head to Arthur Avenue in the Bronx for authentic Italian restaurants at less than half the price of those in Little Venice.

Breakfast

If you stay somewhere with a free breakfast, eat smart. Don't eat sugary cereals or white flour rich pastries if you don't want to be hungry an hour later. Before leaving your hotel or checking out, find some fresh fruit, water, and granola in the fitness centre or coffee in the lobby or business centre. If your hotel doesn't have free breakfast, don't take it. You can always eat cheaper outside.
Johny's Luncheonette has the best cheap breakfast we found. Here you can pick up pancakes for less than $3.

Visit supermarkets at discount times.

You can get a 50 per cent discount around 5 pm at the Whole Foods supermarkets on fresh produce. The cheaper the supermarket, the less discounts you will find, so check Whole Foods supermarkets at 5 pm before the discount supermarkets. Some items are also marked down due to sell-by date after the lunchtime rush so its also worth to check in around 3 pm.

Use delivery services on the cheap.

Take advantage of local offers on food delivery services. Many of the newest ones are flush with Venture Capital Money and hence are offering major discounts for new customers. These include GoPuff, FridgeNoMore and Gorilla.

Most established platforms including Seamless and Door Dash offer $10 off the first order in New York.

SNAPSHOT: How to enjoy a $5,000 trip to New York for $350

(full breakdown at the end of the guide)

Stay	Travelling in peak season:
	1. Last-minute hotels via priceline.com express deals
	2. Stay in a private room in a Airbnb if you want privacy and cooking facilities.
	3. Stay in hostels if you want to meet over travellers.
	4. University accommodation in summer time
	5. Housesit.
	6. Nap York - $20 a night sleep pod.
	Travelling in low season
	1. Last minute five-star hotels.
	You can find Private room on airbnb for $22 a night in the city. Here is the link to a perfect https://www.airbnb.com/rooms/653612940490299787 If you're visiting during vacation times look at student dorm rooms - https://www.universityrooms.com/en-GB/city/newyork/home/
Eat	From bagels to corned-beef sandwiches, Italian fine dining to curbside fast food, and from sashimi to sauerkraut, the breadth of cuisines is matched only by the range of prices. But you don't have to spend huge amounts to eat well. Budget an average of $5 - $15 for each meal.
Move	Use the Subway. It costs $32 for a weeks unlimited travel.
See	Free museums, Staten Island Ferry, a Broadway show, markets, street art and so much more. totalling $20 in entrance fees when you follow our tips on how to visit free or cheap)
Experience	Michelin-star restaurants, rooftop bars and broadway.
Total	US$350

Unique bargains I love in New York

New York has the reputation of being among the most luxurious and expensive destinations in the world. Fortunately, some of the best things in life are free (or almost free). There are a plethora of amazing free tours, free concerts, cheap theatre and film screenings, pay-what-you-wish nights at museums, city festivals, plus loads of green space to escape the urban sprawl.

Chelsea market and Gotham Food Hall are great for cheap eats. Also, it's always a good idea to picnic in Washington square park and Central Park (really any park). Murray's Cheese shop is near Washington square and you could get delicious grilled cheese or cheese/meat plate and bread and wine to take to the park - it makes for a lovely afternoon. Plus there are usually free shows in Bryant park and Central Park.

The first thing you should do when you arrive is check https://www.timeout.com/newyork/things-to-do/things-to-do-in-new-york-today to see what free events are on. Many entice people to come with free food and drink. Even the most reluctant bargain hunter can be successful in New York..

Take your student card

New York offers hundreds of student discounts. If you're studying buy an ISIC card - International Student Identity Card. It's a great investment because its valid in 133 countries and covers 150,000 discounts including many hundreds in New York.

Senior discounts

Nearly every major museum, attraction and The MTA offers reduced fares for seniors age 65.

How to use this book

Google and TripAdvisor are your on-the-go guides while traveling, a travel guide adds the most value during the planning
phase, and if you're without Wi-Fi. Always download the google
map for your destination - having an offline map will make using
this guide much more comfortable. For ease of use, we've set the
book out the way you travel, booking your flights, arriving, how to
get around, then on to the money-saving tips. The tips we or-
dered according to when you need to know the tip to save money, so free tours and combination tickets feature first. We priori-
tized the rest of the tips by how much money you can save and
then by how likely it was that you could find the tip with a google
search. Meaning those we think you could find alone are nearer
the bottom. I hope you find this layout useful. If you have any
ideas about making Super Cheap Insider Guides easier to use,
please email me philgattang@gmail.com

A quick note on How We Source Super Cheap Tips
We focus entirely on finding the best bargains. We give each of
our collaborators $2,000 to hunt down never-before-seen deals.
The type you either only know if you're local or by on the ground
research. We spend zero on marketing and a little on designing
an excellent cover. We do this yearly, which means we just keep
finding more amazing ways for you to have the same experience
for less.

Now let's get started with juicing the most pleasure from your trip
to New York with the least possible money!

OUR SUPER CHEAP TIPS...

Here are out specific tips to enjoy a $5,000 trip to New York for $350

How to Find Super Cheap Flights to New York

Luck is just an illusion. Anyone can find incredible flight deals. If you can be flexible you can save huge amounts of money. In fact, the biggest tip I can give you for finding incredible flight deals is simple: find a flexible job. Don't despair if you can't do that theres still a lot you can do. The following pages detail the exact method I use to consistently find cheap flights to New York.

Book your flight to New York on a Tuesday or Wednesday

Tuesdays and Wednesdays are the cheapest days of the week to fly. You can take a flight to New York on a Tuesday or Wednesday for less than half the price you'd pay on a Thursday Friday, Saturday, Sunday or Monday.

Start with Google Flights (but NEVER book through them)

I conduct upwards of 50 flight searches a day for readers. I use google flights first when looking for flights. I put specific departure but broad destination (e.g Europe) and usually find amazing deals.

The great thing about Google Flights is you can search by class. You can pick a specific destination and it will tell you which time is cheapest in which class. Or you can put in dates and you can see which area is cheapest to travel to.

But be aware Google flights does not show the cheapest prices among the flight search engines but it does offer several advantages

1. You can see the cheapest dates for the next 8 weeks. Other search engines will blackout over 70% of the prices.
2. You can put in multiple airports to fly from. Just use a common to separate in the from input.
3. If you're flexible on where you're going Google flights can show you the cheapest destinations.
4. You can set-up price tracking, where Google will email you when prices rise or decline.

Once you have established the cheapest dates to fly go over to skyscanner.net and put those dates in. You will find sky scanner offers the cheapest flights.

Get Alerts when Prices to New York are Lowest

Google also has a nice feature which allows you to set up an alert to email you when prices to your destination are at their lowest. So if you don't have fixed dates this feature can save you a fortune.

Baggage add-ons

It may be cheaper and more convenient to send your luggage separately with a service like sendmybag.com Often the luggage sending fee is cheaper than what the airlines charge to check baggage. Visit Lugless.-com or luggagefree.com in addition to sendmybag.-com for a quotation.

Loading times

Anyone who has attempted to find a cheap flight will know the pain of excruciating long loading times. If you encounter this issue use google flights to find the cheapest dates and then go to skyscanner.net for the lowest price.

Always try to book direct with the airline

Once you have found the cheapest flight go direct to the airlines booking page. This is advantageous in the current covid cancellation climate, because if you need to change your flights or arrange a refund, its much easier to do so, than via a third party booking agent.

That said, sometimes the third party bookers offer cheaper deals than the airline, so you need to make the decision based on how likely you think it is that disruption will impede you making those flights.

More flight tricks and tips

www.secretflying.com/usa-deals offers a range of deals from the USA and other countries. For example you can pick-up a round trip flight non-stop from from the east coast to johannesburg for $350 return on this site

Scott's cheap flights, you can select your home airport and get emails on deals but you pay for an annual subscription. A free workaround is to download Hopper and set search alerts for trips/ price drops.

Premium service of Scott's cheap flights.
They sometime have discounted business and first class but in my experience they are few and far between.

JGOOT.com has 5 times as many choices as Scott's cheap flights.

kiwi.com allows you to be able to do radius searches so you can find cheaper flights to general areas.

Finding Error Fares
Travel Pirates (www.travelpirates.com) is a gold-mine for finding error deals. Subscribe to their newsletter. I recently found a reader an airfare from Montreal-Brazil for a $200 round trip (mistake fare!). Of course these error fares are always certain dates, but if you can be flexible you can save a lot of money.

Things you can do that might reduce the fare to New York:--
• Use a VPN (if the booker knows you booked one-way, the return fare will go up)
• Buy your ticket in a different currency

How to Find CHEAP FIRST-CLASS Flights to New York

Upgrade at the airport

Airlines are extremely reluctant to advertise price drops in first or business class tickets so the best way to secure them is actually at the airport when airlines have no choice but to decrease prices dramatically because otherwise they lose money. Ask about upgrading to business or first-class when you check-in. If you check-in online look around the airport for your airlines branded bidding system. For example KLM at Amsterdam have terminals where you can bid on upgrades.

Use Air-miles

When it comes to accruing air-miles for American citizens **Chase Sapphire Reserve card** ranks top. If you put everything on there and pay it off immediately you will end up getting free flights all the time, aside from taxes.

Get 2-3 chase cards with sign up bonuses, you'll have 200k points in no time and can book with points on multiple airlines when transferring your points to them.

Please note, this is only applicable to those living in the USA. In the Bonus Section we have detailed the best air-mile credit cards for those living in the UK, Canada, Germany, Austria, Spain and Australia.

How many miles does it take to fly first class?

First class from Bangkok to Chicago (one way) costs 180,000 miles.

Cheapest route to NYC from Europe

At the time of writing Norwegian are flying to New York for around $260 return from Paris.

Arriving

There are three airports in New York and the cheapest way to and from them all is with public transport.
Here's the cheapest method from each airport:

John F. Kennedy International Airport (JFK):

AirTrain JFK: This is a cost-effective option for getting from JFK to the city. The AirTrain connects to the subway system, allowing you to transfer to the A, E, or J subway lines to reach Manhattan. The AirTrain fare is $7.75, and the subway fare is $2.75, making it a total of $10.50.

LaGuardia Airport (LGA):
MTA Bus: You can take the Q70-SBS bus from LaGuardia to Jackson Heights-Roosevelt Ave subway station (where you can transfer to various subway lines). The bus fare is $2.75, and the subway fare is $2.75, totaling $5.50.

Newark Liberty International Airport (EWR):

AirTrain Newark: This connects Newark Airport to the Newark Liberty International Airport Station, where you can catch a NJ Transit or Amtrak train to New York Penn Station. The AirTrain fare is $7.75, and the NJ Transit fare varies but is around $13 one way to Penn Station.

Express Bus: The Newark Airport Express bus operates between Newark Airport and several locations in Manhattan, including Grand Central Station, Bryant Park, and Port Authority Bus Terminal. The fare is approximately $18-$20 one way.

Take a helicopter from the airport to Manhattan

If you're landing at JFK and want the ultimate bougie arrival into Manhattan you can take a helicopter from JKF into Manhattan. blade.com are offering the flight for $195 plus you'll receive three free drinks and obviously a helicopter ride over Manhattan. The average 15-minute ride over Mahanttan is approximately $235 making this a steal. And here's the super cheap part, they are offering 50% discounts. Either use a plugin like 'HONEY' to find a code or google discount code for Blade. This is the last code I found to be working in November 2022 - MATTHEWC002

Need a place to store luggage?
Use stasher.com to find a convenient place to store your luggage cheaply. It provides much cheaper options than airport and train station lockers in New York.

These are some of the cheapest options available, but prices and availability may vary depending on the time of day, demand, and any ongoing promotions or discounts. It's always a good idea to check for updates or changes in transportation options before your trip.

Getting Around

New York City is composed of five boroughs: The Bronx, Brooklyn, Manhattan, Queens, and Staten Island. Brooklyn has the largest population at 2.5 million.

E-scooters/ bike sharing

Like a growing number of cities around the world, New York has a bike-sharing program - . A single ride is $3 or a day pass is $12.

Public transport

Get an unlimited MTA weekly card - $33 - to use the subway. It's the cheapest and easiest way to get around the city. The first underground line of the subway opened on October 27, 1904, Though the city's first official subway line was the IRT, which opened in 1868.

Tips for Riding the New York City Subway

Tips for Riding the New York City Subway

- Check MTA.info for Delays and Detours.
- Avoid Rush Hour 7am to 10am and 4pm to 7pm.
- Use a Metrocard.
- Use the Free Subway to Bus Transfers.
- Before you board check if a Train is Going Uptown or
- Downtown.
- Pickpockets target tourists in New York. Disguise yourself
- as a local by buying a local branded reusable supermarket bag to use as your day bag.

The NYC subway is quite dirty due to the vacuum trains the MTA uses to suck up trash, which they bought in 1997 and 2000, frequently don't run when they're supposed to because they are broken down so often.

INSIDER CULTURAL INSIGHT

As you sit on the subway imagine that one day they will be submerged under the Ocean. As of 2019 2,500 decommissioned subway carriages have been sunk to provide habitats for sea creatures.

Take the ferry
'There are six routes, as well as one seasonal route, connecting 25 ferry piers across all five boroughs. The longest line from the NYC Ferry is: RW. This Ferry route starts from Rockaway (Queens) and ends at Wall St/Pier 11 (Manhattan). It covers over 25 km and has 3 stops." Tickets are $2.75.

Get around for FREE
Use ride sharing service Lyft. Google for a free credit and open a new Lyft account. New York offers up to $50 free credit, which could cover your transport for your whole trip.

Walk – it's the best way to discover New York. Take a different route, and you just might see the City from a whole new angle.

Use public transportation to avoid the hefty cab prices. Take the AirTrain, the airport's public transit line to connect with New York City's subways, buses, and rails. Public transportation is the most affordable way to get to downtown and may be the fastest with traffic.

INSIDER CULTURAL INSIGHT

Manhattan's name originates from its a native history: Man-nahata, or 'island of many hills' in the native Lenape language.

Drive - there's an app called 'Getaround' which allows you to rent a car from $0.19 per minute + more for the Kilometre's but it's cheaper than a car rental and you can do hourly, daily or even weekly packages. You just scan the QR code on the code, hop in and drive.

Below is a chart summarizing the key transportation options and their respective fares:

Transportation Mode	Fare
Subway (Single Ride)	$2.75
Subway (7-day Pass)	$33
Subway (30-day Pass)	$127
Bus (Single Ride)	$2.75
Staten Island Ferry	Free
NYC Ferry	$2.75
Citi Bike	$12/day (approx.)
Car Rentals	Varies

Orientate yourself with this free tour

Forget exploring New York by wandering around aimlessly. Always start with a free organised tour if one is available. Nothing compares to local advice, especially when travelling on a budget. I gleamed many of our super cheap tips from local guides and locals in general, so start with a organised tour to get your bearings and ask for their recommendations for the best cheap eats, the best bargains, the best markets, the best place for a particular street eat. Perhaps some of it will be repeated from this guide, but it can't hurt to ask, especially if you have specific needs or questions. At the end you should leave an appropriate tip (usually around $5), but nobody bats an eye lid if you are unable or unwilling to do so, tell them you will leave a good review and always give them a little gift from home - I always carry small Vienna fridge magnets and I always tip the $5, but it is totally up to you.

The best free tour is with the greeters - locals who show you NYC. You can choose the neighborhood you want to tour, just book here: www.bigapplegreeter.org Reserve at least four weeks in advance to avoid disappointment.

There are 19 more free Tours available including Central Park. Lower Manhattan. 9/11 Memorial and World Trade Center. Greenwich Village. Food Tour of Greenwich Village. SoHo. The Brooklyn Bridge and The High Line:

INSIDER HISTORICAL INSIGHT
Standard street signs are green, look out for brown signs they indicate historic districts.

INSIDER MONEY SAVING TIP

If you have more time consider Geocaching. This is where you hunt for hide-and-seek containers. You need a mobile device to follow the GPS clues in New York. A typical cache is a small, waterproof container with a logbook where you can leave a message or see various trinkets left by other cache hunters. Build your own treasure hunt by discovering geocaches in New York.

There are also three more totally free tours you can take:

- **Brooklyn Bridge Park Conservancy Tours**: The Brooklyn Bridge Park Conservancy offers free walking tours of Brooklyn Bridge Park led by volunteer guides. These tours cover the park's history, ecology, and design, and they are open to all without any expectation of tipping.
- **Central Park Conservancy Tours**: The Central Park Conservancy offers free guided tours of Central Park led by volunteer guides. These tours explore different areas of the park, including its history, architecture, and landscapes. While donations to support the Conservancy's work are appreciated, they are not required for participation.
- **NYC Parks Tours**: NYC Parks offers free guided tours of various parks and landmarks throughout the city. These tours are led by park staff or volunteer guides and cover topics such as history, nature, and art. While tips may be accepted, they are not mandatory.

Consider the New York Pass

If you plan to hit all the major attractions in New York the New York pass can save you money on: Top of the Rock, Empire State Building, 9/11 Memorial Museum and 97 more attractions. Starting at $150 for adults for one day it is not cheap. However if you got up early to do the top attractions it works out at $19 per attraction. The key benefit is as well as saving money, you save time on queuing.

Buy the pass online and save 30% off the retail price. You can download the New York Pass mobile ticket. Consult the website to see if it matches your needs

If you're travelling with kids

- Washington Square Park has amazing playgrounds for toddlers and older children.
- Bryant Park puts on juggling lessons, free theatre and puppet shows.
- Brooklyn Bridge Park has (as mentioned) free kayaking in the summer and SPARK Children's Museum free on Thursdays from 1 pm - 6 pm.
- There is also the historic Jane's Carousel. Though the carousel does cost $2,
- Hudson River Park has many free activities for kids.
- SeaGlass Carousel in Battery park is only $5.50.

New York's Biggest Attractions

Here are the money-saving tips, practical things you need to know, and insider history for each of NYC's unmissable sights:

Statue of Liberty:

- Money-saving tip: Instead of booking expensive guided tours, opt for ferry tickets that provide access to Liberty Island and Ellis Island, where you can explore at your own pace.
- Practical tip: Purchase ferry tickets online in advance to skip the long lines at the ticket counter.
- Insider history: The Statue of Liberty was a gift from France to the United States and has been a symbol of freedom and democracy since its dedication in 1886.

Times Square:

- Practical tip: Avoid eating or shopping in Times Square as prices tend to be higher due to its popularity among tourists.
- Insider history: Times Square was originally known as Longacre Square until 1904 when The New York Times moved its headquarters to the area, prompting the name change.

Metropolitan Museum of Art:

- Money-saving tip: Take advantage of the museum's pay-what-you-wish admission policy for New York State residents and students.
- Practical tip: Plan your visit strategically to avoid crowds, such as arriving early in the morning or on weekdays.
- Insider history: The Metropolitan Museum of Art, often referred to as "the Met," was founded in 1870 and is one of the largest and most prestigious art museums in the world.

Brooklyn Bridge:

- Money-saving tip: Walk or bike across the Brooklyn Bridge for free to enjoy stunning views of the Manhattan skyline and Brooklyn waterfront.
- Practical tip: Start your walk from the Brooklyn side for the best photo opportunities.
- Insider history: The Brooklyn Bridge, completed in 1883, was the first steel-wire suspension bridge constructed and became an engineering marvel of its time.

Rockefeller Center:

- Money-saving tip: Visit Rockefeller Center during the holiday season to see the iconic Christmas tree and ice-skating rink without paying for attractions.
- Practical tip: Take advantage of the free views from the Top of the Rock observation deck by dining at the Rockefeller Center's restaurants.

- Insider history: Rockefeller Center was built during the Great Depression and was intended to be a "city within a city" with offices, shops, and entertainment venues.

Grand Central Terminal:

- Money-saving tip: Skip the pricey restaurants inside Grand Central Terminal and opt for the outside food vendors and eateries.
- Practical tip: Take a free guided tour of Grand Central Terminal to learn about its fascinating history and architecture.
- Insider history: Grand Central Terminal opened in 1913 and is one of the world's most famous train stations, known for its Beaux-Arts architecture and iconic celestial ceiling in the main concourse.

The Battery:

- Money-saving tip: Enjoy the stunning views of Ellis Island and the Statue of Liberty from The Battery for free, instead of paying for a ferry tour.
- Practical tip: Take a leisurely stroll through The Battery's gardens and monuments to soak in its rich history and peaceful atmosphere.
- Insider history: The Battery is a historic park that dates back to the 17th century and was once home to a fort that protected New York City during its early years.

Theatre District:

- Money-saving tip: Purchase discounted Broadway tickets at the TKTS booth in Times Square for same-day performances.
- Practical tip: Explore Off-Broadway shows for more affordable theater experiences with equally impressive performances.
- Insider history: The Theatre District, also known as Broadway, has been the epicenter of American theater since the early 20th century, hosting world-renowned productions and performances.

Liberty Island:

- Money-saving tip: Avoid purchasing tickets for guided tours of Liberty Island and instead opt for audio tours or explore independently for a more budget-friendly option.
- Practical tip: Arrive early in the day to avoid long lines for the ferry to Liberty Island and maximize your time exploring the Statue of Liberty and its museum.
- Insider history: Liberty Island has been home to the Statue of Liberty since its dedication in 1886, serving as a symbol of freedom and democracy for millions of immigrants arriving in the United States.

9/11 Memorial:

- The 9/11 Memorial and Museum offers free timed admission on Tuesday evenings from 5:00 PM to 8:00 PM.
- Practical tip: Reserve your tickets online in advance to secure your preferred time slot and avoid waiting in line at the ticket counter.

- Insider history: The 9/11 Memorial and Museum honors the victims of the 1993 and 2001 terrorist attacks on the World Trade Center, offering a poignant and reflective experience for visitors.

SoHo, Manhattan:

- Money-saving tip: Explore SoHo's art galleries and boutique shops without making purchases by admiring the elegant cast-iron facades and cobblestone streets.
- Practical tip: Visit SoHo during weekdays to avoid the crowds and enjoy a more relaxed shopping and dining experience.
- Insider history: SoHo, short for "South of Houston Street," underwent a transformation from industrial warehouses to a trendy shopping district in the 1970s, becoming known for its iconic architecture and artistic community.

Coney Island:

- Money-saving tip: Consider visiting Coney Island during weekdays or early mornings to avoid peak crowds and find discounts on tickets for rides and attractions.
- Practical tip: Pack your own snacks and drinks to save money on concessions while enjoying the boardwalk and beach.
- Insider history: Coney Island has been a popular summer destination since the late 19th century, boasting iconic attractions like the Cyclone roller coaster and the Nathan's Famous hot dog eating contest.

American Museum of Natural History:

- Money-saving tip: Take advantage of the museum's suggested admission policy to pay what you can afford, although some special exhibits may require additional fees.
- Practical tip: Plan your visit ahead of time by checking the museum's website for information on current exhibitions, special events, and interactive experiences.
- Insider history: The American Museum of Natural History was founded in 1869 and has grown to become one of the largest and most renowned natural history museums in the world, featuring exhibits on dinosaurs, space exploration, and biodiversity.

Solomon R. Guggenheim Museum:

- Money-saving tip: Look for discounted admission days or consider purchasing tickets online in advance to skip the lines and potentially save on ticket prices.
- Practical tip: Take advantage of free guided tours or audio guides to learn about the museum's collection and architecture during your visit.
- Insider history: Designed by Frank Lloyd Wright and opened in 1959, the Guggenheim Museum is renowned for its unique spiral rotunda and modern art collection, showcasing works by artists like Picasso, Kandinsky, and Pollock.

The Plaza:

- Money-saving tip: While staying at The Plaza may be a splurge, consider visiting for a drink or afternoon tea to experience the hotel's iconic ambiance without breaking the bank.
- Practical tip: Check online for special promotions or packages that may offer discounted rates for dining or spa services at The Plaza.
- Insider history: Built in 1907, The Plaza has long been synonymous with luxury and elegance, hosting notable guests like The Beatles, F. Scott Fitzgerald, and Eloise, the beloved children's book character.

Greenwich Village:

- Money-saving tip: Explore Greenwich Village on foot to discover hidden gems, street art, and historic landmarks without spending a dime.
- Practical tip: Visit Washington Square Park for free outdoor performances, people-watching, and photo opportunities with the iconic arch.
- Insider history: Greenwich Village became a bohemian enclave in the early 20th century and played a central role in the counterculture movements of the 1950s and 1960s, nurturing the Beat Generation, folk music revival, and LGBTQ rights activism.

Bryant Park:

- Money-saving tip: Attend free events and activities in Bryant Park throughout the year, including outdoor movie screenings, yoga classes, and ice skating in the winter.

- Practical tip: Bring a picnic blanket and snacks to enjoy a leisurely afternoon in the park, surrounded by lush greenery and iconic New York City landmarks.
- Insider history: Originally known as Reservoir Square, Bryant Park was redesigned in the 1930s as a public space and cultural hub, hosting concerts, art exhibitions, and literary events for residents and visitors alike.

Flatiron Building:

- Money-saving tip: Take a self-guided walking tour of the Flatiron District to admire the neighborhood's historic architecture, including the iconic Flatiron Building, without spending a dime.
- Practical tip: Visit Madison Square Park nearby for a peaceful retreat and photo opportunities with views of the Flatiron Building and Empire State Building.
- Insider history: Completed in 1902, the Flatiron Building was one of the tallest skyscrapers in New York City at the time of its construction and remains a beloved symbol of the city's architectural and cultural heritage.

DUMBO:

- Money-saving tip: Take advantage of happy hour deals at DUMBO's trendy cafes and restaurants for discounted drinks and snacks with stunning views of the Manhattan skyline.
- Practical tip: Visit during the week to avoid the crowds and enjoy a leisurely stroll along the cobblestone streets and waterfront parks.

- Insider history: DUMBO, short for "Down Under the Manhattan Bridge Overpass," was once a bustling industrial area and has since transformed into a vibrant neighborhood known for its artistic community and breathtaking views.

Little Italy:

- Money-saving tip: Skip the tourist traps and explore the side streets of Little Italy to discover authentic Italian bakeries and trattorias offering delicious food at affordable prices.
- Practical tip: Visit during the annual Feast of San Gennaro festival to experience the neighborhood's lively atmosphere, street vendors, and live entertainment.
- Insider history: Little Italy was once home to a large Italian immigrant population and is now a nostalgic enclave known for its red-checkered tablecloths, cannoli, and espresso.

Union Square:

- Money-saving tip: Shop for fresh produce, artisanal goods, and affordable meals at the Union Square Greenmarket, held four days a week.
- Practical tip: Take a leisurely stroll through Union Square Park to admire the statues, fountains, and seasonal plantings while people-watching.
- Insider history: Union Square has been a gathering place for activists, artists, and New Yorkers of all walks of life since the 19th century, hosting rallies, protests, and cultural events.

Lower East Side:

- Money-saving tip: Explore the Lower East Side's vibrant street art scene and eclectic boutiques for unique finds and souvenirs without breaking the bank.
- Practical tip: Visit during the day to explore the neighborhood's historic landmarks and cultural institutions, then return at night for live music, comedy shows, and nightlife.
- Insider history: The Lower East Side was once home to waves of immigrants from Eastern Europe, Asia, and Latin America, shaping its diverse and dynamic character.

Washington Square Park:

- Money-saving tip: Pack a picnic lunch and enjoy it in Washington Square Park while listening to live music or watching street performers for free entertainment.
- Practical tip: Visit the park in the evening for stunning views of the iconic Washington Square Arch illuminated against the night sky.
- Insider history: Washington Square Park has been a cultural hub and gathering place for artists, activists, and students since the 19th century, hosting rallies, concerts, and impromptu performances.

Financial District:

- Money-saving tip: Take a self-guided walking tour of the Financial District to admire its historic landmarks, including Federal Hall and Trinity Church, without paying for guided tours.

- Practical tip: Visit the Charging Bull sculpture and nearby Fearless Girl statue for iconic photo opportunities without spending money.
- Insider history: The Financial District is the historic heart of New York City's financial industry, home to Wall Street, the New York Stock Exchange, and the Federal Reserve Bank.

Intrepid Sea, Air & Space Museum:

- Money-saving tip: Check for discounted admission tickets online or through local attractions passes to save on entry fees to the Intrepid Museum.
- Practical tip: Plan your visit during special events or exhibit openings for unique experiences and interactive activities.
- Insider history: The Intrepid Sea, Air & Space Museum is housed aboard the USS Intrepid aircraft carrier, which served in World War II and the Vietnam War, and offers visitors the chance to explore military history and technological innovation.

Meatpacking District:

- Money-saving tip: Explore the galleries and public art installations in the Meatpacking District's historic warehouses for free cultural experiences.
- Practical tip: Visit the High Line park, an elevated linear park built on a former railway line, for scenic views of the neighborhood and Hudson River.
- Insider history: The Meatpacking District was once a hub of meatpacking and manufacturing industries and has since evolved into a trendy neighborhood

known for its nightlife, art scene, and upscale boutiques.

Manhattan Bridge:

- Money-saving tip: Walk or bike across the Manhattan Bridge for free to enjoy panoramic views of the East River, Brooklyn, and Manhattan's skyline.
- Practical tip: Explore the surrounding neighborhoods of Chinatown and DUMBO for diverse cultural experiences and local eateries.
- Insider history: The Manhattan Bridge, completed in 1909, is one of the city's iconic bridges and a vital transportation link connecting Manhattan and Brooklyn.

Pro tip: Official City Audio Guides

The official tourism website of New York City may offer free audio guides for download or streaming. These guides typically cover popular attractions such as Central Park, Times Square, and the Statue of Liberty, providing informative commentary on each location.

Visit these incredible Free Museums

To make sure everybody has access to culture many of New York's top museums are free or have times when you can visit for free. Here are the best of the crop:

These museums are Always Free
National Museum of the American Indian - part of the Smithsonian Institution and is committed to advancing knowledge and understanding of the Native cultures of the Western Hemisphere—past, present, and future—through partnership with Native people and others

National September 11 Memorial

Museum at FIT - collection of garments & accessories

Hamilton Grange - preserves the relocated home of U.S. Founding Father Alexander Hamilton
American Folk Art Museum
Nicholas Roerich Museum Admission by Donation
American Museum of Natural History
Brooklyn Museum
Museum of the City of New York
Brooklyn Historical Society - Free or Pay-What-You-Wish on Certain Days
The Queens Museum is also free (need to book a timed entry though). Corona Park is site of 1962 World's Fair and the museum is one of the fair "leftovers". The diorama and art exhibits are cool.

These museums are Free at selected times:

MoMA – 4–9pm Friday
MET - FREE every Friday from 4 pm-8 pm
Rubin Museum of Art – 6–10pm Friday
Asia Society & Museum – 6–9pm Friday, September to June Japan Society – 6–9pm Friday
Frick Collection – 2–6pm Wednesday & 6–9pm first Friday of month
New Museum of Contemporary Art – 7–9pm Thursday
New-York Historical Society – 6–8pm Friday
Jewish Museum – 5–8pm Thursday and Saturday
Guggenheim Museum – 5:45–7:45pm Saturday -
Take the elevator to the top floor of the Guggenheim and make your way down the spiral
ramp, taking in highlights of 20th
century art along the way.
Whitney Museum of American Art – 7–10pm Friday Neue Galerie – 6–8pm first Friday of month

Museum of Natural History is free for the last hour of every day

Visit NYC's Top Free Historical Sights

- Ellis Island (New York Harbor)
  - Gracie Mansion (Upper East Side)
  - Merchant's House Museum (NoHo)
  - Jane's Carousel (Brooklyn)
  - Historic Richmond Town (Staten Island)

FREE TOUR ALERT: Cooper Hewitt Smithsonian Design Museum offers Free tours are at 11:30am and 1:30pm on weekdays, and at 1pm and 3pm on weekends.

Go to a Broadway show on the cheap

The origins of Broadway history in New York begun in 1750 when a theater company was opened on Nassau Street. This theater was large enough to hold 280 people and mainly put on Shakespearian plays and ballad operas. Over three centuries later over 15 million people flock to see broadway shows. With the average ticket price costing $124, its not cheap. Luckily there are eight ways for you to buy super cheap tickets.

By buying your tickets on the day of the show you can get them 50% cheaper. There are two ways to do this:

1. Download the Today Tix app
2. Go to the TKTS booth right in Times Square that opens twice a day and sells cheap broadway shows for that day. The big shows like Wicked and Book of Mormon won't have but you can find good seats for other major performances from $15.

3. Many shows also offer rush tickets (Most productions hold back a percentage of tickets to sell on the day) as online digital lotteries now, where you enter the day or two before and hope for the best. Here's a list: https://www.playbill.com/article/broadway-rush-lottery-and-standing-room-only-policies-com-116003

4. Rush tickets at the box office. Show up at the productions box office 10am on Monday to Saturday and noon on Sundays to get deeply discounted 'rush tickets'.

5. 'Not all Broadway shows offer Standing Room Only tickets, but for the ones that do, the average cost of these deeply discounted tickets is about $25' Tickets Are Usually For Sold-Out Performances Only. Here's a list of shows which offer standing tickets - https://www.nytix.com/discount-broadway-tickets

If same-day tickets don't suit you there are other options.

1. If you're open to any show, try Broadway Roulette. You pick the day, it picks the show. You can get major productions from $25.

2. Broadway For Broke People has options the day ahead of when you want to go to a Broadway show.

3. The Will-Call Club is a theater seat filling service that offers discount tickets* to Broadway. You pay $20 for a yearly membership. It's probably worth the fee if you're in the US for a longer time.

Eat at a Cheap Michelin starred restaurant

Finding a Michelin-starred restaurant in NYC that won't break the bank can be a challenge, but it's not impossible. Here are a few options known for offering exceptional dining experiences at relatively affordable prices:

- **Junoon**: Located in the Flatiron District, Junoon is a Michelin-starred Indian restaurant offering modern takes on traditional dishes. While it's known for its upscale ambiance and innovative cuisine, Junoon also offers a lunch prix-fixe menu starting at around $28 per person, making it a more budget-friendly option for experiencing Michelin-starred dining.
- **Cafe China**: This Michelin-starred restaurant in Midtown serves up authentic Sichuan cuisine in a cozy and unassuming setting. Prices at Cafe China are reasonable, with lunch specials starting at

around $15 and dinner entrees ranging from $20 to $30. Diners can enjoy flavorful dishes like dan dan noodles, mapo tofu, and spicy cumin lamb without breaking the bank.

- **Hunan Slurp**: Nestled in the East Village, Hunan Slurp offers Michelin-recommended Hunanese cuisine with a focus on noodles and seafood. While it's not a traditional Michelin-starred restaurant, Hunan Slurp has garnered praise for its bold flavors and affordable prices, with most dishes priced under $20.
- **Laut**: Another Michelin-recommended gem, Laut serves up Malaysian, Thai, and Singaporean cuisine in a casual yet elegant atmosphere. While it's not officially Michelin-starred, Laut offers high-quality dishes at reasonable prices, with lunch specials starting at around $10 and dinner entrees ranging from $15 to $30.
- **Casa Enrique**: Located in Long Island City, Casa Enrique is the only Michelin-starred Mexican restaurant in NYC. Despite its accolades, Casa Enrique remains relatively affordable, with lunch specials starting at around $15 and dinner entrees ranging from $20 to $30. Diners can enjoy authentic Mexican flavors in a laid-back atmosphere without breaking the bank.

Do free wine tastings

'The Finger Lakes area is the main New York wine region for the production of Riesling, Long Island and Hamptons area are known for their Merlot and Cabernet Franc.' Thanks to the variety of nearby vineyards there are lots of shops which offer free wine tastings. Here are the best:

- September Wines - in the Lower East Side
- Chelsea Wine Vault in the Chelsea Market
- Union Square Wines in Union Square
- Nolita Wine Merchants - near Little Italy
- Astor Wines in the East Village

Walk The High Line

The High Line was a freight rail line, in operation from 1934 to 1980. Today it is an elevated linear park, greenway and rail trail created on a former New York Central Railroad. It provides some of the best views of the city and is great for snapping photos. You start at Gansevoort Street in the Meatpacking District and end at West 34th Street, between 10th and 12th Avenues.

Take the FREE Staten Island Ferry

The best way to see The Statue of Liberty is with the 25 minute FREE ride on the Staten Island ferry. Leaving from South Ferry Terminal in Lower Manhattan, on it you can enjoy breathtaking views of Lower Manhattan's skyline and an even better one of the Statue of Liberty. Be aware of scammers trying to sell tickets, the ferry is free.
From May to October, you can also take a FREE ferry over to Governors Island, a car-free island with great views. For more adventure, take out a free kayak, available in the Hudson River Park,
Brooklyn Bridge Park and Red Hook.

Visit this Cheap alternative to the Empire State Building

This famous art-deco skyscraper opened in 1930, it is no longer New York's tallest building but it has one of the best sunset views. Plus the newly added LED lights create more than 16 million color possibilities. If you go up to the top it will costs you $39. The best time to visit is sunset.

If you don't want to pay the $39 for the view, head to The Spyglass Rooftop Bar. The view from top is unmatched in New York. It is not the highest, but it is an intimate view and quite lovely. Plus, no one really goes there anymore so it's not touristy and it will cost you the price of a soda.

Walk across the Brooklyn Bridge

Brooklyn Bridge is a suspension/cable-stay
hybrid bridge connecting Manhattan and Brooklyn. It is one
of the oldest suspension bridges in United States (completed in 1883) and a first steel-wire suspension bridge in the
world.Jump on a 4, 5 or 6 train to Brooklyn Bridge. You will
be at the Manhattan end of New York's most famous bridge.
Afterwards take a break in the Empire Fulton Ferry State
Park on the Brooklyn side.

Go to a top TV show for free

Fancy being in the audience of famous TV shows? Many are taped in New York City Including: The Late Show with Stephen Colbert, The Drew Barrymore Show, The Daily Show with Trevor Noah and The Tonight Show Starring Jimmy Fallon give out free audience tickets. Either go to TKTS booth in Times Square on Mondays or Tuesdays and you should find somebody heckling about free tickets or log on to https://www.tvtaping.com/ to reserve your spot. https://www.nycgo.com/articles/live-tv-show-tapings-and-tickets also posts calls for audience members.

Take in breathtaking Tram Views

Roosevelt Island Aerial Tram costs about $6 return and a free bus takes you around Roosevelt. The jaw-dropping 360-degree view of New York City is best enjoyed at night and the tram runs past midnight every night.

If you'd like to see another breathtaking night view of New York take the East River Ferry just $2.75. It runs past 9 pm every night.

Do some free high-powered Stargazing

From April to October, members of the Amateur Astronomers Association bring high-powered telescopes to various parks in NYC. For times and parks visit: https://www.aosny.org/

Visit New York Public Library

Built in 1911, it is the largest marble structure ever built in the United States. The New York Public Library is monumental and gorgeous inside. It is also an awesome place to go if you are looking for a quiet to escape NYC's crazy. My favourite place to read is the Rose Reading Room on the 3rd floor. There's also free wifi and charging sockets.

Go to The Bronx Zoo!

The Bronx Zoo opened its doors to the public in 1899. It is home to over 4,000 animals. **Wednesday's are free at the Bronx Zoo**, they do ask you to consider making a donation to help in caring for the 600 species of animals. This zoo emphasises the emotional connection and is a great way to spend a Wednesday afternoon. The food options are over-prices, so bring your own snacks if you want them.

Watch free perfor-mances

Manhattan

SummerStage takes place from June through early September, and features over 100 free performances at 17 parks. Shakespeare in the Park, held also in Central Park. Top actors like Meryl Streep and Al Pacino have taken the stage in years past! Prospect Park has its own open-air summer concert and events series. Celebrate Brooklyn.

Go to a Free outdoor cinema

In summertime you can see free films at the River to River Festival (www.rivertorivernyc.com; at Hudson River Park in Manhattan and at Brooklyn Bridge Park www.brooklyn-bridgepark.org

Chck out the free HBO Bryant Park Summer Film Festival (www.bryantpark.org; hmid-Jun–Aug) screenings on Monday nights.

Hear Gospel Music
Many churches, especially in Harlem and Brooklyn, open up their doors on Wednesdays and Sundays for religious services with incredible gospel music.

Watch Free Live music

BAMcafe in Brooklyn has free concerts (world music, R&B, jazz, rock) on select Friday and Saturday nights. In Harlem, Marjorie Eliot opens her home for free jazz jams on Sunday. If you like jazz, visit Blue Note, Birdland or Village Vanguard. The atmosphere is electrifying during the live sets. Look at https://www.bam.org/programs/bamcafe-live to see when they have no cover charge days.

Explore the markets

Exploring markets in New York City is not only a fun and eye-opening experience but also an affordable way to immerse yourself in the local culture. While you may encounter persistent vendors, visiting these markets won't cost you a dime, and you'll have the opportunity to discover a diverse array of goods and culinary delights.

Chinatown is a prime destination for market browsing, where you can stroll through bustling streets lined with vendors selling everything from fresh produce to unique trinkets. Don't miss out on the chance to sample cheap yet delicious treats like dumplings, pork buns, and hand-pulled noodles, which are sure to tantalize your taste buds without breaking the bank.

In addition to Chinatown, there are several other markets worth exploring across the city. The Brooklyn Flea, LIC Flea Market in Queens, and Union Square Greenmarket are just a few examples of vibrant markets where you can find an eclectic mix of goods, ranging from vintage clothing to artisanal food products.

For those with a penchant for Latin American cuisine, the Red Hook Food Vendors are a must-visit. Located in Brooklyn, this outdoor market features a diverse selection of authentic dishes that are sure to satisfy your cravings for flavorful fare.

If you're in the mood for fresh produce and baked goods at discount prices, be sure to check out Stiles Farmers Market. This neighborhood grocer offers a wide variety of locally sourced products that are both affordable and of high quality.

For bargain hunters seeking designer goods, Century 21 is a treasure trove of deals. With its discounted prices on a wide range of fashion items, this department store is a favorite among budget-conscious shoppers. Just be prepared for crowds, especially on weekends.

For a taste of history, consider visiting La Marqueta, also known as the Park Avenue Retail Market. Dating back to 1936, this market was designed to provide indoor space for vendors previously operating in open-air pushcart markets. While its original purpose may have shifted over the years, La Marqueta remains a vibrant hub of activity where you can find an assortment of goods and culinary delights.

To save even more money while shopping in New York City, keep an eye out for sample sales in the Garment District. These sales offer deep discounts on designer goods, with savings of up to 90% off retail prices. Look for flyers and sidewalk billboards advertising upcoming sales, and you may just score a fantastic deal on your next fashion find.

Go to an Auction

Founded in 1766, Christie's is a famous British auction house. Christie's New York is always free to visit. They have guest lectures, a beautiful gallery with diverse exhibits all for FREE!
Address: Rockefeller Center

Watch Free comedy

New York City is renowned for its vibrant and dramatic atmosphere, where every corner seems to exude a sense of excitement and energy. Amidst the hustle and bustle of city life, there's a thriving comedy scene that offers a plethora of free shows each month, providing laughter and entertainment to locals and visitors alike. Here are some of the best comedy shows that you can catch across NYC, Brooklyn, and Queens:

- **The Lantern Comedy Club**: Located in the heart of the city, The Lantern Comedy Club is a hotspot for stand-up comedy enthusiasts. With a lineup of talented comedians and a lively atmosphere, it's the perfect place to unwind and enjoy some laughs with friends.
- **"Hot Soup" at Irish Exit**: Every Tuesday at 8pm, Irish Exit in Midtown East plays host to "Hot Soup," a hilarious comedy show that features a rotating lineup of top-notch comedians. Grab a drink and prepare to be entertained by some of the city's funniest performers.
- **"Gandhi, Is That You" at Lucky Jack's**: Head to Lucky Jack's in the Lower East Side on Wednesdays at 9pm for "Gandhi, Is That You," a comedy show that promises plenty of laughs and good times. With its intimate setting and talented lineup, it's a must-visit for comedy enthusiasts.
- **"Whiplash" at Upright Citizens Brigade**: On Mondays at 11pm, comedy aficionados flock to the Upright Citizens Brigade in Chelsea for "Whiplash," a renowned comedy showcase that features both up-and-coming talent and established comedians. Prepare to be amazed by the sheer talent on display.

- **"Broken Comedy" at Bar Matchless**: Located in Greenpoint, Bar Matchless is home to "Broken Comedy," a popular comedy show that showcases some of the city's most innovative and hilarious comedians. With its laid-back vibe and welcoming atmosphere, it's a favorite among locals and visitors alike.
- **Open Mic Night at Legion Bar**: If you're feeling adventurous, why not try your hand at comedy? Head to Legion Bar in Williamsburg for their open mic night, where aspiring comedians can take the stage and test out their material in front of a supportive audience.

For the latest show times and updates, be sure to visit free-standupnyc.com, your go-to source for all things comedy in New York City.

As you navigate the vibrant streets of New York City, it's important to keep in mind some insider cultural insights. While New Yorkers are known for their friendliness and willingness to engage in conversation, there are certain topics that are considered off-limits. Avoid asking someone you don't know about their rent or salary, as it's considered impolite and invasive. Instead, focus on enjoying the vibrant culture and diverse experiences that the city has to offer, and you're sure to have an unforgettable time in the Big Apple.

Chill out in Central Park

After many years of debate over the location, the park's construction finally began in 1857, based on the winner of a park design contest, the "Greensward Plan," Affectionately known as 'The Lungs of New York', Central Park is one of the most beautiful parts of New York and you can see why locals love it so much.

Stretching from 59th St in Midtown Manhattan to 110th St in Harlem its a refuge from the cities chaos. It has free wifi, so you can still stay on, if you want to.

INSIDER MONEY SAVING TIP

If central Park is overcrowded head to Governors Island its home to a 25-foot hill that offers a 360-degree view of the city's harbour.

INSIDER MONEY SAVING TIP

Sara Roosevelt Park – bordered by Canal, Chrystie, Houston, and Forsyth streets – is a hidden sanctuary for kids with basketball, volleyball, and handball courts, soccer fields, five playgrounds, and a community garden.

Pumphouse Park

If you visit in spring or summer then floral Pumphouse Park is a must-see. But even in the colder months the park along the Hudson River will be filled with families playing in the snow.

Go Church Hopping

New York City's churches stand as majestic monuments to both architectural grandeur and spiritual significance. Beyond their awe-inspiring facades, these sacred spaces house a wealth of exquisite art, artifacts, and other priceless treasures. What's more, many of these churches welcome visitors to explore their general areas free of charge, offering a glimpse into their rich history and cultural heritage.

One such iconic landmark is Trinity Church Wall Street, a historic Episcopal parish located in the heart of Lower Manhattan. Founded in 1697, Trinity Church boasts stunning

Gothic Revival architecture and is renowned for its beautiful interior adorned with intricate stained glass windows and ornate furnishings. Visitors can wander through the church's tranquil grounds and marvel at its timeless beauty, all without spending a dime.

St. Patrick's Cathedral, a beloved symbol of New York City, is another must-visit destination for those seeking spiritual solace and architectural splendor. Situated on Fifth Avenue in Midtown Manhattan, this neo-Gothic masterpiece captivates visitors with its towering spires, intricate marble carvings, and breathtaking rose windows. Step inside to admire the cathedral's soaring nave and tranquil chapels, where moments of quiet reflection await amid the hustle and bustle of the city.

Grace Church, nestled in the vibrant neighborhood of Greenwich Village, is revered for its striking Gothic Revival design and rich cultural heritage. Dating back to the mid-19th century, this historic Episcopal parish boasts a stunning interior adorned with intricate woodwork, colorful stained glass, and awe-inspiring vaulted ceilings. Visitors can attend a worship service or simply explore the church's serene surroundings, soaking in the atmosphere of reverence and tranquility.

Hillsong Church Manhattan, part of the global Hillsong Church network, offers a contemporary worship experience in the heart of New York City. With its modern architecture and vibrant community, Hillsong Church welcomes visitors from all walks of life to come together in worship and fellowship. Attend a Sunday service or special event to experience the uplifting music and inspiring message of hope.

The Brooklyn Tabernacle, located in the heart of downtown Brooklyn, is renowned for its dynamic worship services and powerful ministry outreach. Housed in a historic former theater, this vibrant evangelical church welcomes visitors to join in its passionate worship gatherings and experience the transformative power of faith. From uplifting music to heartfelt sermons, the Brooklyn Tabernacle offers a spiritual oasis amidst the bustling cityscape.

As you explore these sacred spaces, it's important to show respect for their religious significance and cultural heritage. While many of these churches welcome tourists and visitors, remember to observe any posted guidelines and be mindful of ongoing worship services or events. By embracing the opportunity to journey through New York City's rich tapestry of faith and architecture, you'll gain a deeper appreciation for the city's diverse cultural landscape.

Thrift shop

Exploring thrift stores in NYC is like embarking on a treasure hunt, with the promise of discovering unique finds at unbeatable prices. However, with stiff competition among bargain hunters, it's essential to strategize for success. Arriving early and bringing snacks for sustained energy levels are key tactics for maximizing your thrift shopping experience. Here are some of the top thrift stores in NYC where you can uncover hidden gems:

- **Lot Less Closeouts** - Located at 206 W 40th St, Lot Less Closeouts is a haven for thrifty shoppers seeking great deals on a variety of items. From clothing and accessories to household goods and electronics, this store offers a diverse selection at discounted prices.
- **Artists and Fleas at Chelsea Market** - Nestled within the iconic Chelsea Market at 88 Tenth Ave, Artists and Fleas is a must-visit destination for vintage enthusiasts. Explore rows of stalls showcasing handmade crafts, vintage clothing, and unique treasures from local artisans.

- **Philip Williams Posters** - Situated at 122 Chambers St, Philip Williams Posters is a hidden gem specializing in rare and collectible posters. Whether you're a movie buff, music lover, or art enthusiast, you'll find an eclectic array of posters spanning various genres and eras.
- **Housing Works Thrift Shop** - With multiple locations throughout the city, Housing Works Thrift Shop is a nonprofit organization dedicated to supporting individuals affected by HIV/AIDS. Shop for clothing, furniture, books, and more while supporting a worthy cause.

When scouting for thrift stores, it's wise to target locations in affluent areas with lower foot traffic from low-income residents. If you're unsure where to start, a simple Google search for the most expensive neighborhoods in NYC can provide valuable insights. From there, use Google Maps to locate thrift stores in these areas, starting with the most upscale establishments and gradually exploring middle-tier options. You'll be amazed at the hidden treasures waiting to be unearthed in these unexpected places.

In addition to clothing and household items, thrift stores can also be a goldmine for literary enthusiasts seeking rare first editions and collectible books. Make a pilgrimage to Westsider Rare & Used Books, where you'll find a curated selection of fiction, art books, children's literature, and rock music albums. Whether you're a seasoned collector or just starting your literary journey, you never know what hidden treasures await you on the shelves of this beloved bookstore.

Go Book Shopping

Bookoff offers a huge range of paperback books for low prices.

Address: 49 W 45th Street.

Explore NYC Street art

The roots of modern street art can be traced back to New York City's graffiti boom, which began in the 1960s and evolved through the 1970s, reaching its peak in the 1980s with the iconic spray-painted full-car subway train murals that adorned the Bronx. Today, the city continues to be a vibrant canvas for urban artists, with an array of incredible artworks waiting to be discovered. Here are some of the best places to spot these mesmerizing urban canvases:

- **Welling Court Mural Project, Astoria**: This outdoor gallery in Astoria features an ever-changing collection of murals created by local and international artists. From vibrant abstract designs to thought-provoking political statements, there's something for everyone to appreciate here.
- **First Street Green Art Park, East Village**: Located in the heart of the East Village, this community-run

art park serves as a platform for emerging and established artists to showcase their work. Visitors can admire a diverse range of murals, sculptures, and installations that reflect the neighborhood's rich cultural heritage.

- **The Bowery Wall, Nolita**: Situated on Houston Street in Nolita, the Bowery Wall is an iconic spot for street art enthusiasts. Renowned artists from around the world are invited to paint large-scale murals on this massive outdoor canvas, resulting in breathtaking works of art that captivate passersby.
- **Freeman Alley, Lower East Side**: Tucked away in the Lower East Side, Freeman Alley is a hidden gem known for its vibrant street art and eclectic atmosphere. Stroll through this narrow passageway to discover a diverse array of murals, graffiti tags, and wheatpaste posters that showcase the neighborhood's creative spirit.
- **The Bushwick Collective, Bushwick**: As one of the city's most prolific street art destinations, Bushwick is home to the Bushwick Collective, an outdoor gallery featuring an extensive collection of murals by local and international artists. From colorful portraits to abstract compositions, the streets of Bushwick are alive with creativity.
- **Graffiti Hall of Fame, East Harlem**: Pay a visit to East Harlem's Graffiti Hall of Fame to see some of the city's most iconic graffiti artworks. Established in the 1980s, this outdoor gallery celebrates the rich history and cultural significance of graffiti art, showcasing the work of legendary artists alongside emerging talents.
- **Tuff City, Bronx**: Explore the streets of the Bronx to discover Tuff City, a renowned graffiti hotspot that attracts artists from far and wide. From vibrant lettering to intricate murals, the Bronx is a treasure trove of urban art waiting to be explored.

- **Coney Art Walls, Coney Island**: Take a trip to Coney Island to experience the vibrant energy of the Coney Art Walls, an outdoor exhibition featuring large-scale murals by some of the world's most celebrated street artists. Set against the backdrop of the iconic boardwalk, these colorful artworks add an extra layer of excitement to the Coney Island experience.

In addition to these outdoor galleries, New York City is home to a number of indoor spaces where street art enthusiasts can admire curated collections in a gallery setting. Some notable galleries include:

- **Centre-fuge Public Art Project's rotating gallery**: This innovative project transforms empty storefronts and construction sites into temporary galleries, showcasing the work of local artists in unexpected urban spaces.
- **Lower East Side's Freeman Alley**: In addition to its outdoor murals, Freeman Alley is also home to several galleries that specialize in street art and contemporary urban art. Visitors can explore these galleries to discover new talent and cutting-edge artworks.
- **Graffiti Hall of Fame's Latin American art**: In addition to its outdoor mural space, the Graffiti Hall of Fame also features a gallery that highlights the work of Latin American artists. Visitors can explore exhibitions that celebrate the diversity and cultural heritage of the graffiti art movement.
- **'Love Vandal' by Nick Walker's**: Nick Walker is a renowned street artist known for his iconic "Love Vandal" series, which explores themes of love, rebellion, and urban culture. His works can be found in galleries and exhibitions across the city, offering art

enthusiasts the chance to experience his unique vision up close.

- **Welling Court Mural Project, Queens' premier street-art gallery**: In addition to its outdoor murals, the Welling Court Mural Project also features a gallery space that showcases the work of participating artists. Visitors can explore the gallery to learn more about the artists and their creative process.

Hopefully, you know agree with me, that New York City is a treasure trove of free experiences!

We will now look at each borough best freebies - uncovering free museums, parks, events, and more in every corner of the city. From world-class art exhibitions to scenic waterfront parks, from vibrant street festivals to historic landmarks, there's something for everyone to enjoy without opening their wallets.

Best of Manhattan Freebies

- **Stroll through Central Park**: Enjoy a leisurely walk through Central Park, admiring the lush greenery, picturesque bridges, and scenic views of the skyline. Starting price: Free.
- **Visit the High Line**: Explore the elevated High Line park, which offers stunning views of the city, art installations, and lush greenery. Starting price: Free.
- **Window shopping on Fifth Avenue**: Take a stroll along Fifth Avenue and indulge in some high-end window shopping, admiring the designer boutiques and luxury stores. Starting price: Free.
- **Explore Grand Central Terminal**: Marvel at the iconic architecture of Grand Central Terminal, with its celestial ceiling, elegant Vanderbilt Hall, and bustling concourse. Starting price: Free.
- **Enjoy street food**: Treat yourself to delicious street food from food carts and vendors scattered throughout Manhattan, offering a variety of cuisines at affordable prices. Starting price: $5-$10.
- **Visit the New York Public Library**: Explore the majestic halls and historic reading rooms of the New York Public Library, one of the city's most iconic landmarks. Starting price: Free.
- **Take a ferry ride to Staten Island**: Enjoy panoramic views of the Statue of Liberty, Ellis Island, and the Manhattan skyline on a free ferry ride to Staten Island. Starting price: Free.
- **Attend a free concert or performance**: Check out free concerts, live music performances, and cultural events happening at venues like Bryant Park, Lincoln Center, and Rockefeller Center. Starting price: Free.

- **Picnic in Bryant Park**: Relax and unwind in Bryant Park, where you can enjoy a picnic on the lawn, play lawn games, or simply people-watch. Starting price: Free.
- **Explore Chelsea Market**: Wander through the bustling halls of Chelsea Market, browsing gourmet food shops, artisanal vendors, and unique boutiques. Starting price: Free to explore; costs vary for food purchases.
- **Walk across the Brooklyn Bridge**: Take a scenic walk across the iconic Brooklyn Bridge, enjoying panoramic views of the Manhattan skyline and the East River. Starting price: Free.
- **Visit the Museum of Modern Art (MoMA) on Fridays**: Explore world-class art collections at the Museum of Modern Art (MoMA) for free on Friday evenings from 5:30 pm to 9:00 pm. Starting price: Free on Fridays; regular admission is $25.
- **Explore the Chelsea Galleries**: Wander through the Chelsea art galleries, where you can view contemporary art exhibitions and discover emerging artists. Starting price: Free.
- **Attend a free yoga class in the park**: Participate in free outdoor yoga classes held in parks across Manhattan, offering a rejuvenating experience amidst nature. Starting price: Free.
- **Take a self-guided architectural tour**: Explore Manhattan's diverse architecture on a self-guided tour, admiring iconic landmarks and historic buildings throughout the city. Starting price: Free.
- **Visit the 9/11 Memorial and Reflecting Pools**: Pay your respects at the 9/11 Memorial and Reflecting Pools, honoring the victims of the September 11, 2001, terrorist attacks. Starting price: Free.
- **Explore the Cloisters**: Discover medieval European art and architecture at the Cloisters museum, located in Fort Tryon Park overlooking the Hudson River.

Starting price: Pay-what-you-wish for New York residents; suggested admission for others is $25.

- **Attend a free rooftop bar event**: Enjoy breathtaking views of the city skyline at free rooftop bar events hosted by various hotels and venues in Manhattan. Starting price: Free entry; drinks may be purchased separately.
- **Walk along the Hudson River Greenway**: Take a scenic stroll or bike ride along the Hudson River Greenway, offering stunning views of the river, parks, and skyline. Starting price: Free.
- **Visit the Oculus at the World Trade Center**: Experience the futuristic architecture of the Oculus transportation hub and shopping mall at the World Trade Center site. Starting price: Free to explore; costs vary for shopping and dining.

Best of Queens Free-bies

- **Visit Flushing Meadows-Corona Park**: Explore the expansive Flushing Meadows-Corona Park, home to iconic landmarks like the Unisphere and Queens Museum. Starting price: Free.
- **Picnic at Gantry Plaza State Park**: Enjoy stunning views of the Manhattan skyline and the East River while picnicking at Gantry Plaza State Park in Long Island City. Starting price: Free.
- **Wander through Queens Botanical Garden**: Stroll through the beautiful Queens Botanical Garden, featuring themed gardens, walking paths, and seasonal flower displays. Starting price: Free admission on Wednesdays from 3 pm to 6 pm, otherwise $6 for adults.
- **Explore Socrates Sculpture Park**: Discover contemporary outdoor sculptures and art installations at Socrates Sculpture Park in Long Island City. Starting price: Free.
- **Attend a free concert at Forest Hills Stadium**: Check out free concerts and events held at Forest Hills Stadium, a historic outdoor venue in Queens. Starting price: Free for select events; prices vary for ticketed concerts.
- **Take a self-guided food tour of Queens**: Explore the diverse culinary scene of Queens by embarking on a self-guided food tour, sampling international cuisines from local eateries. Starting price: Varies based on food purchases; many affordable options available.
- **Visit the Queens Night Market**: Experience a vibrant outdoor market featuring food vendors, artisanal goods, and live performances at the Queens

Night Market in Flushing Meadows-Corona Park. Starting price: Free entry; prices vary for food purchases.

- **Walk along the Rockaway Beach Boardwalk**: Take a leisurely stroll along the Rockaway Beach Boardwalk, enjoying panoramic views of the Atlantic Ocean and the beachfront scenery. Starting price: Free.
- **Explore Queens Museum**: Visit the Queens Museum located in Flushing Meadows-Corona Park, showcasing art exhibitions and cultural programs. Starting price: Pay-what-you-wish on Sundays; suggested donation of $8 for adults.
- **Attend a free yoga class in the park**: Participate in free outdoor yoga classes held in parks across Queens, offering relaxation and rejuvenation amidst nature. Starting price: Free.
- **Visit the Louis Armstrong House Museum**: Explore the former home of jazz legend Louis Armstrong in Corona, Queens, featuring exhibits on his life and legacy. Starting price: $12 for adults; free admission for children under 4.
- **Discover Astoria Park**: Spend the day at Astoria Park, enjoying outdoor activities such as picnicking, jogging, tennis, and waterfront views along the East River. Starting price: Free.
- **Attend a free cultural event at Queens Theatre**: Enjoy free cultural events, performances, and screenings at Queens Theatre located in Flushing Meadows-Corona Park. Starting price: Free for select events; prices vary for ticketed performances.
- **Explore the Queens County Farm Museum**: Visit the Queens County Farm Museum, one of the oldest working farms in New York City, featuring farm animals, historic buildings, and seasonal events. Starting price: Free admission; donations appreciated.
- **Take a self-guided tour of historic neighborhoods**: Explore historic neighborhoods in Queens such as Jackson Heights, Forest Hills, and

Sunnyside, admiring architectural landmarks and cultural diversity. Starting price: Free.

- **Relax at Spa Castle Premier 57**: Treat yourself to a day of relaxation and pampering at Spa Castle Premier 57 in College Point, featuring saunas, pools, and hydrotherapy baths. Starting price: Weekday admission starts at $65.
- **Take a scenic bike ride along the Queens Greenway**: Cycle along the Queens Greenway, a network of bike paths and green spaces connecting neighborhoods throughout the borough. Starting price: Free if you bring your own bike; Citi Bike rentals available at affordable rates.
- **Attend a free outdoor movie screening**: Watch a movie under the stars at a free outdoor screening hosted by various parks and organizations in Queens. Starting price: Free.
- **Explore Jamaica Bay Wildlife Refuge**: Discover the natural beauty of Jamaica Bay Wildlife Refuge, home to diverse bird species, marshlands, and nature trails. Starting price: Free.
- **Visit the Museum of the Moving Image**: Explore the Museum of the Moving Image in Astoria, featuring exhibitions on film, television, and digital media. Starting price: $15 for adults; free admission on Fridays from 4 pm to 8 pm.

Best of Brooklyn Freebies

- **Walk across the Brooklyn Bridge**: Take a scenic stroll across the iconic Brooklyn Bridge, enjoying panoramic views of the Manhattan skyline and the East River. Starting price: Free.
- **Visit Prospect Park**: Explore the vast expanse of Prospect Park, featuring meadows, woodlands, lakes, and recreational facilities such as the Prospect Park Zoo and LeFrak Center at Lakeside. Starting price: Free.
- **Picnic at Brooklyn Bridge Park**: Enjoy stunning views of the Brooklyn Bridge and the Manhattan skyline while picnicking at Brooklyn Bridge Park, which offers waterfront promenades, recreational piers, and lush green spaces. Starting price: Free.
- **Attend a free concert at Prospect Park Bandshell**: Experience live music performances and cultural events at the Prospect Park Bandshell during the summer months. Starting price: Free for select events.
- **Explore Brooklyn Botanic Garden**: Wander through the beautiful Brooklyn Botanic Garden, featuring themed gardens, blooming flowers, and seasonal events such as the Cherry Blossom Festival. Starting price: Free admission on Fridays before noon; otherwise $18 for adults.
- **Visit the Brooklyn Museum**: Explore the Brooklyn Museum, home to an extensive art collection spanning various cultures and time periods. Starting price: Pay-what-you-wish on the first Saturday of the month from 5 pm to 8 pm; otherwise $16 for adults.
- **Take a self-guided street art tour in Bushwick**: Explore the vibrant street art scene in Bushwick by

taking a self-guided tour of colorful murals and graffiti artworks adorning the neighborhood's walls and buildings. Starting price: Free.

- **Attend a free film screening at Brooklyn Bridge Park**: Watch movies under the stars at Brooklyn Bridge Park's Movies with a View series, featuring classic films and contemporary favorites with the Manhattan skyline as a backdrop. Starting price: Free.
- **Discover Brooklyn Heights Promenade**: Take a leisurely walk along the Brooklyn Heights Promenade, offering breathtaking views of the Manhattan skyline, the Brooklyn Bridge, and the Statue of Liberty. Starting price: Free.
- **Explore Coney Island Boardwalk**: Experience the lively atmosphere of Coney Island Boardwalk, featuring amusement rides, games, arcades, and iconic attractions like the Wonder Wheel and Nathan's Famous hot dogs. Starting price: Free to explore; costs vary for rides and attractions.
- **Visit Green-Wood Cemetery**: Explore the historic Green-Wood Cemetery, known for its picturesque landscapes, ornate mausoleums, and the final resting places of notable figures in New York City history. Starting price: Free to explore; guided tours available for a fee.
- **Attend a free outdoor yoga class**: Participate in free outdoor yoga classes held in parks and public spaces across Brooklyn, offering relaxation and rejuvenation amidst nature. Starting price: Free.
- **Explore Brooklyn Heights**: Wander through the charming streets of Brooklyn Heights, admiring historic brownstone homes, tree-lined avenues, and stunning views of the Manhattan skyline. Starting price: Free.
- **Discover Brooklyn Flea Market**: Browse unique vintage finds, handmade crafts, artisanal foods, and antiques at the Brooklyn Flea Market, held at various

locations in Brooklyn throughout the year. Starting price: Free to explore; costs vary for purchases.

- **Visit the New York Aquarium**: Explore the underwater world at the New York Aquarium in Coney Island, featuring marine exhibits, interactive displays, and animal encounters. Starting price: Pay-what-you-wish on Wednesdays from 3 pm to last entry; otherwise $26.95 for adults.
- **Explore Brooklyn Navy Yard**: Take a guided tour of the Brooklyn Navy Yard, a former naval shipyard turned industrial park, featuring historic buildings, waterfront views, and innovative businesses. Starting price: Free to explore; guided tours available for a fee.
- **Attend a free outdoor concert at Brooklyn Navy Yard**: Enjoy free outdoor concerts and performances at the Brooklyn Navy Yard during the summer months, featuring live music, food vendors, and family-friendly activities. Starting price: Free.
- **Visit Brooklyn Public Library**: Explore the Brooklyn Public Library, featuring a vast collection of books, multimedia resources, and cultural programs for visitors of all ages. Starting price: Free.
- **Take a scenic bike ride along the Brooklyn Greenway**: Cycle along the Brooklyn Greenway, a network of bike paths and waterfront trails connecting neighborhoods from Greenpoint to Bay Ridge. Starting price: Free if you bring your own bike; Citi Bike rentals available at affordable rates.
- **Attend a free cultural event at BRIC House**: Experience free cultural events, exhibitions, and performances at BRIC House in Downtown Brooklyn, featuring contemporary art, music, film, and theater. Starting price: Free for select events.

Best of The Bronx freebies

- **Explore the Bronx Zoo**: Spend a day exploring the Bronx Zoo, one of the largest metropolitan zoos in the world, featuring a diverse collection of animals and immersive exhibits. Starting price: Pay-what-you-wish on Wednesdays; otherwise $39.95 for adults.
- **Visit the New York Botanical Garden**: Wander through the New York Botanical Garden, featuring 250 acres of lush landscapes, themed gardens, and seasonal flower displays. Starting price: Pay-what-you-wish on Wednesdays and from 9 am to 10 am on Saturdays; otherwise $23 for adults.
- **Discover the Bronx Museum of the Arts**: Explore the Bronx Museum of the Arts, showcasing contemporary art exhibitions, cultural programs, and community outreach initiatives. Starting price: Free admission.
- **Walk along the Bronx River Greenway**: Take a scenic walk or bike ride along the Bronx River Greenway, a network of trails and parks following the Bronx River from Westchester County to the East River. Starting price: Free.
- **Picnic at Pelham Bay Park**: Enjoy a picnic at Pelham Bay Park, the largest park in New York City, featuring beaches, woodlands, hiking trails, and recreational facilities. Starting price: Free.
- **Attend a free concert at Bronx Borough Hall**: Experience live music performances and cultural events at Bronx Borough Hall, featuring local artists and musicians. Starting price: Free.
- **Visit Wave Hill**: Explore Wave Hill, a public garden and cultural center overlooking the Hudson River,

featuring gardens, greenhouses, and outdoor art installations. Starting price: $10 admission for adults; free on Tuesdays and Saturdays from 9 am to 12 pm.

- **Explore City Island**: Spend the day exploring City Island, a quaint waterfront community known for its seafood restaurants, marinas, and nautical charm. Starting price: Free to explore; costs vary for dining and activities.
- **Attend a free outdoor movie screening**: Watch movies under the stars at a free outdoor movie screening hosted by various parks and organizations in The Bronx. Starting price: Free.
- **Take a self-guided tour of historic landmarks**: Discover historic landmarks in The Bronx such as the Edgar Allan Poe Cottage, Woodlawn Cemetery, and the Grand Concourse on a self-guided tour. Starting price: Free.
- **Visit the Bronx River Art Center**: Explore the Bronx River Art Center, featuring contemporary art exhibitions, workshops, and community events. Starting price: Free admission.
- **Take a scenic walk along the Grand Concourse**: Stroll along the Grand Concourse, a wide boulevard lined with Art Deco buildings, cultural institutions, and historic landmarks. Starting price: Free.
- **Attend a free fitness class at a local park**: Participate in free fitness classes and exercise programs held at parks and recreation centers across The Bronx, including yoga, Zumba, and boot camps. Starting price: Free.
- **Visit the Hall of Fame for Great Americans**: Explore the Hall of Fame for Great Americans, a historic colonnade honoring prominent Americans throughout history, located on the campus of Bronx Community College. Starting price: Free.
- **Attend a free cultural event at Hostos Center for the Arts & Culture**: Experience free cultural events,

performances, and exhibitions at Hostos Center for the Arts & Culture, featuring theater, dance, music, and visual arts. Starting price: Free for select events.

- **Take a self-guided street art tour in Hunts Point**: Discover colorful murals and graffiti artworks in Hunts Point by taking a self-guided street art tour of the neighborhood. Starting price: Free.
- **Visit the Bronx Victory Memorial**: Pay tribute to veterans at the Bronx Victory Memorial, a monument commemorating Bronx residents who served in World War I. Starting price: Free.
- **Attend a free event at BronxWorks: The Living Room**: Participate in free community events, workshops, and performances at BronxWorks: The Living Room, a cultural and social space in the South Bronx. Starting price: Free for select events.
- **Explore Van Cortlandt Park**: Discover the natural beauty of Van Cortlandt Park, featuring forests, wetlands, hiking trails, and recreational facilities such as golf courses and horseback riding. Starting price: Free.
- **Attend a free cultural event at Pregones Theater**: Experience free cultural events and performances at Pregones Theater in the South Bronx, featuring theater productions, live music, and community gatherings. Starting price: Free for select events.

Best of Staten Island Freebies

- **Visit Snug Harbor Cultural Center and Botanical Garden**: Explore the picturesque grounds of Snug Harbor, featuring historic buildings, botanical gardens, art exhibitions, and cultural events. Starting price: Free to explore; donations appreciated.
- **Take a scenic walk along the Staten Island Greenbelt**: Enjoy a leisurely walk or hike through the Staten Island Greenbelt, a network of trails and natural areas offering stunning views of forests, wetlands, and wildlife. Starting price: Free.
- **Picnic at Clove Lakes Park**: Relax and unwind at Clove Lakes Park, where you can enjoy a picnic by the lakes, paddleboat rentals, and scenic walking paths. Starting price: Free.
- **Explore Historic Richmond Town**: Step back in time at Historic Richmond Town, a living history village showcasing 400 years of Staten Island's history through historic buildings, demonstrations, and special events. Starting price: $8 for adults; free for children under 12.
- **Visit the Staten Island Museum**: Discover the art, culture, and natural history of Staten Island at the Staten Island Museum, featuring exhibitions, educational programs, and family-friendly activities. Starting price: $8 for adults; free for children under 12.
- **Attend a free concert at Snug Harbor**: Experience free outdoor concerts and performances at Snug Harbor Cultural Center and Botanical Garden during the summer months, featuring live music, dance, and theater. Starting price: Free.
- **Explore Fort Wadsworth**: Visit Fort Wadsworth, a historic military fort overlooking the entrance to New

York Harbor, featuring scenic overlooks, walking trails, and panoramic views of the Verrazano-Narrows Bridge. Starting price: Free.

- **Take a scenic drive along the Staten Island waterfront**: Enjoy a scenic drive along the Staten Island waterfront, offering views of the New York Harbor, the Statue of Liberty, and the Manhattan skyline. Starting price: Free.
- **Attend a free outdoor movie screening**: Watch movies under the stars at a free outdoor movie screening hosted by various parks and organizations in Staten Island. Starting price: Free.
- **Visit the National Lighthouse Museum**: Learn about the history and significance of lighthouses at the National Lighthouse Museum in St. George, featuring exhibits, artifacts, and educational programs. Starting price: $8 for adults; free for children under 12.
- **Explore the Alice Austen House**: Visit the Alice Austen House, a historic waterfront home and museum dedicated to the pioneering photographer Alice Austen. Starting price: $5 suggested donation for adults; free for children under 18.
- **Take a ferry ride to Governors Island**: Take a free ferry ride to Governors Island from the Staten Island Ferry Terminal in St. George, where you can explore historic buildings, parks, and art installations. Starting price: Free ferry ride; costs vary for activities on the island.
- **Attend a free cultural event at the Snug Harbor Performing Arts Center**: Experience free cultural events and performances at the Snug Harbor Performing Arts Center, featuring live music, dance, theater, and family-friendly entertainment. Starting price: Free for select events.
- **Visit the Tibetan Museum**: Explore the Jacques Marchais Museum of Tibetan Art, a unique cultural institution featuring Tibetan art, architecture, and arti-

facts in a serene hilltop setting. Starting price: $6 for adults; free for children under 12.

- **Take a self-guided tour of historic sites in St. George**: Discover historic sites in St. George such as the St. George Theatre, St. George's Episcopal Church, and the Staten Island September 11 Memorial on a self-guided walking tour. Starting price: Free.
- **Visit the Greenbelt Nature Center**: Explore the Greenbelt Nature Center, a gateway to the Staten Island Greenbelt, featuring interactive exhibits, educational programs, and guided nature walks. Starting price: Free.
- **Attend a free cultural event at the Garibaldi-Meucci Museum**: Experience free cultural events and exhibitions at the Garibaldi-Meucci Museum, celebrating the legacies of Italian patriots Giuseppe Garibaldi and Antonio Meucci. Starting price: Free for select events.
- **Explore Staten Island's beaches**: Spend a day relaxing on the sandy shores of Staten Island's beaches, including South Beach, Midland Beach, and Cedar Grove Beach. Starting price: Free.
- **Take a self-guided tour of the Staten Island Greenbelt Conservancy**: Discover the natural beauty and biodiversity of the Staten Island Greenbelt on a self-guided tour of the Greenbelt Conservancy's nature trails and parks. Starting price: Free.
- **Visit the Staten Island Children's Museum**: Explore interactive exhibits and hands-on activities at the Staten Island Children's Museum, offering educational fun for children and families. Starting price: $8 for adults and children; free for infants under 1 year old.

Escape the crowds

The title may sound like an oxymoron in bustling New York City, which welcomed a staggering 67 million visitors in 2019. However, despite this massive influx of people, there are still tranquil spots to be discovered amidst the urban hustle and bustle. For those who find themselves easily overwhelmed by crowds, strategic planning and exploration of lesser-known gems can offer moments of serenity amid the city's vibrant energy.

One key strategy for avoiding crowds is to visit popular attractions early in the day, before the peak influx of visitors occurs. Typically, the busiest times are between 11 am and 5 pm, so early risers can enjoy these landmarks in a more serene atmosphere. By getting an early start, you can beat the crowds and fully appreciate the beauty of iconic sites like Times Square, Central Park, or the Statue of Liberty without feeling overwhelmed by throngs of people.

Fortunately, New York City is also home to several hidden gems that offer respite from the hustle and bustle of tourist-packed areas. These lesser-known spots provide a peaceful escape where visitors can unwind and recharge away from the city's frenetic pace. Here are some of the best quiet spots to explore:

The Morgan Library and Museum: Once the private library of financier J.P. Morgan, this architectural gem offers free admission on Fridays from 7 pm to 9 pm. Stepping inside, visitors are transported to a world of elegance and sophistication, surrounded by exquisite works of art and rare manuscripts.

Jamaica Bay Wildlife Refuge: Located in Queens, this expansive wildlife reserve is a haven for nature lovers seeking tranquility amidst the urban landscape. Accessible via public transportation, the refuge boasts serene walking trails, scenic overlooks, and abundant birdwatching opportunities.

Community Gardens: Escape the city's hustle and bustle by exploring one of New York's community gardens, such as 6th and Avenue B, Creative Little Garden, or La Plaza Cultural. These hidden oases offer lush greenery, vibrant blooms, and a peaceful atmosphere for relaxation and reflection.

Greenacre Park: Tucked away between 2nd and 3rd Avenue in Manhattan, Greenacre Park is a hidden gem known for its stunning waterfall feature. Despite its central location, this privately-owned park provides a tranquil retreat from the surrounding urban landscape, offering a peaceful ambiance for visitors to enjoy.

By seeking out these quiet corners of the city, visitors can experience a different side of New York—one characterized by tranquility, natural beauty, and a sense of calm amidst the bustling metropolis. Whether you're strolling through a serene garden or marveling at rare manuscripts in a historic library, these hidden gems offer moments of peace and solitude in the heart of the city that never sleeps.

Get something totally for free

You could furnish an entire apartment pretty decently with all the things people are giving away in New York.

If you find you need to buy something, whether that be a charger or torch in New York check free stuff in New York sites before you buy. You can often find incredible freebies here that will cost you only the time to pick them up. Here is the best free stuff group in New York: https://www.facebook.com/groups/freestuffinnyc/

Not super cheap but loved

SUMMIT One Vanderbilt

'The Summit Ascent ticket prices range from $53-$69. This ticket type provides general admission to the Summit One Vanderbilt observatory as well as a thrilling glass elevator journey in the Ascent elevator that travels over 1,200 feet in the airThe best time to visit the Summit One Vanderbilt is early morning or one hour before sunset. Early morning you'll bump into the least crowds and one hour before sunset, you can catch the best views and capture great photos.'

The Empire State Building and Top of the Rock are included for free on all tourist passes so if observation decks are high on your list of must-sees, buying a tourist pass is a cheaper way to visit them.

NYC Food and Drink hacks

Unlocking the secrets to affordable dining in the concrete jungle of NYC can be a game-changer for budget-conscious travelers. Here are some food and drink hacks to help you navigate the city's culinary landscape without breaking the bank:

Happy Hour Feasts: Dining out in New York can be a drain on your wallet, but don't despair! Take advantage of happy hour specials, typically starting around 4:00 PM and lasting until 8:00 PM or even closing time at some establishments. Score deals like prix-fixe menus, half-price starters, $1 oysters, or 20% off the food menu at select restaurants. It's a savvy way to indulge in delicious fare without the hefty price tag.

All-You-Can-Eat Sushi Extravaganza: Dive into a sushi lover's paradise at A B Sushi Japanese, an all-you-can-eat buffet that defies belief. For just $18 during lunch hours, you can feast on a seemingly endless array of fresh and flavorful sushi. All-you-can-eat buffets are a godsend for travelers looking to fuel up on nutritious meals without breaking the bank. Load up on omega-3-rich fish and savor every bite of your budget-friendly feast.

Budget-Friendly Bites: Craving a flavorful falafel sandwich or juicy chicken kebab? Head to Oasis in Williamsburg, conveniently located near the Bedford Avenue subway stop, where you can snag a mouthwatering falafel sandwich for just $5 or a chicken kebab for $6. For another tantalizing option, check out the green taco truck parked outside Starbucks on Bedford Avenue for the best $8 burrito in NYC (try the steak!).

Bagel Bliss: For a quintessential New York experience, sink your teeth into the best bagel in town at Ess-A-Bagel in Midtown East. Priced at $5, these bagels are bursting with generous fillings that will leave you craving more. It's a must-try moment that encapsulates the essence of NYC's culinary scene.

Hunt for Deals: Keep your eyes peeled for dining deals and discounts on sites like Yelp Deals, Groupon, LivingSocial, and Valpak. You can also score coupons at local hotels, bus or train stations, and even the airport. With a little savvy searching, you'll uncover a treasure trove of savings on your next meal out.

Free Coffee Refills: Stay caffeinated without emptying your wallet by enjoying free refills at Thrillist, a growing coffee chain in NYC that serves up Seattle's Caffé Vita coffee. Indulge in complimentary refills on iced coffee and filter coffees, ensuring that your caffeine fix doesn't break the bank.

Seek Out Free Food: In times of financial hardship, consider visiting The New York City ISKCON Temple for free meals. While it's advisable to reserve this option for extreme circumstances, it's comforting to know that a helping hand is available when needed most.

Must-try New York Street Foods

New York City is a culinary mecca, boasting a plethora of renowned restaurants serving up delectable dishes from around the world. However, there's something truly special about the street food scene in the Big Apple. From savory sandwiches to sweet treats, here are some must-try street foods that capture the essence of New York City:

Let's start with the iconic pastrami sandwich. New York's love affair with pastrami dates back to 1887 when Sussman Volk, a kosher butcher and immigrant from Lithuania, introduced the first pastrami sandwich to the United States. Piled high with tender, smoky pastrami between slices of rye bread, this classic sandwich is a testament to the city's rich culinary history.

Next up, we have baked pretzels. There's nothing quite like biting into a warm, soft pretzel seasoned with salt and served fresh from a street vendor's cart. Whether enjoyed plain or with a side of mustard for dipping, these quintessential New York snacks are a favorite among locals and visitors alike.

Of course, no discussion of New York street food would be complete without mentioning the beloved New York cheesecake. While the cheesecake itself wasn't invented in New York, the city's immigrant bakers perfected a version that became famous around the world. With its creamy texture and rich flavor, New York cheesecake is a dessert lover's dream come true.

Bagels are another street food staple that New Yorkers hold near and dear to their hearts. Believed to have been brought to the city by Eastern European Jewish immigrants in the late 1800s, New York bagels are renowned for their chewy texture and delicious flavor. Whether topped with cream cheese, lox, or a schmear of butter, a freshly baked New York bagel is a true culinary delight.

And let's not forget about New York-style pizza. With its thin crust, gooey cheese, and generous toppings, New York pizza is a slice of heaven on the go. Dating back to 1905 when America's first pizzeria, Lombardi's, opened its doors in Manhattan's Little Italy neighborhood, New York-style pizza has become a beloved street food tradition.

Lastly, we have falafel, tacos, and burritos. These flavorful and portable delights can be found at street food carts on nearly every corner of the city. Whether you're craving Middle Eastern falafel, Mexican tacos, or Tex-Mex burritos, New York's diverse street food scene has you covered.

Cheap Eats

If you tire of eating street foods go to these sit-down restaurants in New York to fill your stomach without emptying your wallet.. Here are the Best Cheap Eats in NYC for Under $5!

All of these local restaurants have mains under $8.

Note: Download the offline map on Google maps, (instructions 1. go to app 2. select offline apps in the left sidebar 3. go to the area you want to download 4. click download). Then simply type the restaurant names in to navigate, add it to your favourites by clicking the star icon so you can see where the cheap eats are when you're out and about to avoid wasting your money at hyped tourist joints)

Manhattan:

Joe's Pizza (Greenwich Village): Known for its classic New York-style pizza slices, Joe's Pizza offers delicious and affordable options. Recommended: Plain cheese slice. Starting price: $2.75 per slice.

Vanessa's Dumpling House (Chinatown): Vanessa's Dumpling House serves up tasty dumplings and other Chinese street food at budget-friendly prices. Recommended: Pork and chive dumplings. Starting price: $1.25 for 4 dumplings.

Mamoun's Falafel (Greenwich Village): Mamoun's Falafel is a beloved spot for Middle Eastern cuisine, serving up flavorful falafel sandwiches and platters. Recommended: Falafel sandwich. Starting price: $3.50 for a falafel sandwich.

Taco Mix (East Harlem): Taco Mix offers authentic Mexican tacos with a variety of fillings at affordable prices. Recommended: Al pastor taco. Starting price: $2.50 per taco.

Xi'an Famous Foods (Various locations): Xi'an Famous Foods specializes in hand-pulled noodles and spicy, flavorful dishes from China's Shaanxi province. Recommended: Spicy cumin lamb noodles. Starting price: $9.75 for a small noodle dish.

Artichoke Basille's Pizza (Various locations): Artichoke Basille's Pizza is known for its indulgent and unique pizza creations. Recommended: Artichoke slice. Starting price: $4.50 per slice.

Pommes Frites (Greenwich Village): Pommes Frites offers Belgian-style fries with a variety of dipping sauces. Recommended: Classic fries with curry ketchup. Starting price: $5.75 for a regular cone.

Gray's Papaya (Upper West Side): Gray's Papaya is famous for its affordable hot dogs and tropical drinks. Recommended: Recession Special (two hot dogs and a drink). Starting price: $5.95 for the Recession Special.

Mamak (Chinatown): Mamak serves Malaysian street food favorites like roti canai and laksa at reasonable prices. Recommended: Roti canai with curry sauce. Starting price: $5.00 for roti canai.

Joe's Steam Rice Roll (Chinatown): Joe's Steam Rice Roll offers a variety of rice rolls filled with ingredients like beef, shrimp, and vegetables. Recommended: Shrimp rice roll. Starting price: $3.75 per rice roll.

Brooklyn:

Di Fara Pizza (Midwood): Di Fara Pizza is a legendary spot known for its meticulously crafted pizzas made with fresh ingredients. Recommended: Classic New York-style pizza slice. Starting price: $5.00 per slice.

Shake Shack (Various locations): Shake Shack is a popular chain serving up delicious burgers, fries, and shakes. Recommended: ShackBurger. Starting price: $6.09 for a single ShackBurger.

Juliana's Pizza (DUMBO): Juliana's Pizza offers classic coal-fired pizzas with a thin crust and fresh toppings. Recommended: Margherita pizza. Starting price: $19.00 for a small Margherita pizza.

Smorgasburg (Various locations): Smorgasburg is a food market featuring a wide variety of vendors offering everything from barbecue and tacos to ice cream and vegan dishes. Recommended: Try different vendors for a diverse culinary experience. Starting price: Varies by vendor, but many items are under $10.

Lucali (Carroll Gardens): Lucali is a cozy pizzeria known for its wood-fired pies and simple, high-quality ingredients. Recommended: Plain pizza pie. Starting price: $24.00 for a plain pizza pie.

Tom's Restaurant (Prospect Heights): Tom's Restaurant is a beloved diner serving classic American comfort food at affordable prices. Recommended: Pancakes with butter and syrup. Starting price: $8.50 for a stack of pancakes.

Sahadi's (Brooklyn Heights): Sahadi's is a Middle Eastern market offering a variety of prepared foods, including falafel, hummus, and stuffed grape leaves. Recommended: Falafel wrap. Starting price: $5.50 for a falafel wrap.

Paulie Gee's Slice Shop (Greenpoint): Paulie Gee's Slice Shop serves up square-shaped Detroit-style pizza with creative toppings. Recommended: Hellboy slice. Starting price: $4.00 per slice.

Di Fara Pizza (Williamsburg): Di Fara Pizza's Williamsburg location offers the same delicious pizzas as the original Midwood location. Recommended: Classic New York-style pizza slice. Starting price: $5.00 per slice.

Fette Sau (Williamsburg): Fette Sau is a barbecue joint serving up smoked meats, sausages, and classic sides. Recommended: Brisket sandwich. Starting price: $12.00 for a brisket sandwich.

Queens:

Arepa Lady (Jackson Heights): Arepa Lady is famous for its delicious Colombian-style arepas filled with various toppings. Recommended: Arepa with cheese. Starting price: $4.00 per arepa.

Queens Night Market (Flushing Meadows-Corona Park): Queens Night Market is a vibrant outdoor market offering a wide variety of international street food from around the world. Recommended: Explore different vendors for a diverse culinary experience. Starting price: Varies by vendor, but many items are under $10.

John Brown Smokehouse (Long Island City): John Brown Smokehouse serves up authentic Kansas City-style barbecue with a variety of smoked meats and classic sides. Recommended: Pulled pork sandwich. Starting price: $9.00 for a pulled pork sandwich.

New World Mall Food Court (Flushing): New World Mall Food Court offers a plethora of options for affordable and delicious Asian cuisine, including dumplings, noodles, and bubble tea. Recommended: Try different stalls for a taste of various Asian cuisines. Starting price: Varies by stall, but many items are under $10.

Lhasa Fast Food (Jackson Heights): Lhasa Fast Food offers authentic Tibetan cuisine, including momos (dumplings) and noodle soups, at budget-friendly prices. Recommended: Beef momos. Starting price: $6.00 for a plate of momos.

Antojitos Doña Fela (Corona): Antojitos Doña Fela serves up delicious and authentic Mexican street food, including tacos, tortas, and quesadillas. Recommended: Al pastor tacos. Starting price: $2.50 per taco.

Biang! (Flushing): Biang! offers hand-pulled noodles and flavorful Chinese dishes inspired by the Shaanxi region. Recommended: Spicy cumin lamb noodles. Starting price: $11.95 for a small noodle dish.

Leo's Latticini (Corona): Leo's Latticini, also known as Mama's of Corona, is a classic Italian deli serving up sandwiches, salads, and fresh mozzarella. Recommended: Italian combo hero. Starting price: $9.50 for a small Italian combo hero.

Arepa Lady (Elmhurst): Arepa Lady's Elmhurst location offers the same delicious Colombian-style arepas as the original Jackson Heights spot. Recommended: Arepa with cheese. Starting price: $4.00 per arepa.

De Mole (Sunset Park): De Mole serves up flavorful Mexican cuisine, including tacos, enchiladas, and mole dishes, at reasonable prices. Recommended: Chicken enchiladas with mole sauce. Starting price: $14.00 for chicken enchiladas.

The Bronx:

Lloyd's Carrot Cake (Woodlawn): Lloyd's Carrot Cake is famous for its delicious, homemade carrot cake in various flavors. Recommended: Classic carrot cake slice. Starting price: $4.00 per slice.

Xochimilco Family Restaurant (Woodstock): Xochimilco Family Restaurant serves authentic Mexican dishes, including tacos, burritos, and enchiladas, at affordable prices. Recommended: Beef tacos. Starting price: $2.00 per taco.

Ceetay (Mott Haven): Ceetay offers a variety of sushi rolls, ramen bowls, and other Asian fusion dishes at reasonable prices. Recommended: Spicy tuna roll. Starting price: $6.00 for a spicy tuna roll.

Charlie's Bar & Kitchen (Mott Haven): Charlie's Bar & Kitchen serves up comfort food classics like burgers, macaroni and cheese, and fried chicken at affordable prices. Recommended: Classic cheeseburger. Starting price: $12.00 for a cheeseburger.

Sofrito White Plains Road (Allerton): Sofrito White Plains Road offers delicious Puerto Rican cuisine, including mofongo, empanadas, and roasted pork, at reasonable prices. Recommended: Chicken empanadas. Starting price: $4.00 for an order of empanadas.

Estrellita Poblana IV (Belmont): Estrellita Poblana IV serves up authentic Mexican dishes, including tacos, tamales, and enchiladas, at budget-friendly prices. Recommended: Beef enchiladas. Starting price: $10.00 for beef enchiladas.

Nicky's Vietnamese Sandwiches (Belmont): Nicky's Vietnamese Sandwiches offers a variety of banh mi sandwiches filled with flavorful ingredients at affordable prices. Recommended: Grilled pork banh mi. Starting price: $6.00 for a banh mi sandwich.

King of Kings (University Heights): King of Kings serves up Dominican-style fast food, including rotisserie chicken, mofongo, and fried plantains, at budget-friendly prices. Recommended: Rotisserie chicken platter. Starting price: $8.00 for a chicken platter.

Lola's Kitchen & Wine Bar (Wakefield): Lola's Kitchen & Wine Bar offers a diverse menu of American comfort food and international cuisine at reasonable prices. Recommended: Grilled cheese sandwich. Starting price: $10.00 for a grilled cheese sandwich.

Tin Marin (Riverdale): Tin Marin serves up Latin American-inspired dishes, including tacos, ceviche, and plantain chips, at affordable prices. Recommended: Chicken tacos. Starting price: $9.00 for chicken tacos.

Nightlife – Bars & Clubs

If you don't go out in New York you'll miss out on some great venues – the clubs and bars make it hard to catch some sleep ibut prices for indulging nocturnal desires aren't cheap. Here are some places to drink on the cheap - all with beers under $4!

• Johnny's Bar
• Rudy's Bar & Grill
• Local 138
• Jimmy's Corner
• Barcelona bar in Hell's Kitchen - Kind of a dive but so en-tertain-ing & they have very cheap drinks for Manhattan.
• Botanica Bar The place is a bit on the dark side, but the prices and happy hour make braving it worth-while.

And Here's a list of top places in each borough of New York City where you can find cheap drinks:

Manhattan:

- **McSorley's Old Ale House (East Village):** McSorley's is one of the oldest bars in NYC, serving up cheap pints of their famous house ale. Recommended: McSorley's Ale. Starting price: $5.50 per pint.
- **Jimmy's Corner (Times Square):** Jimmy's Corner is a classic dive bar with affordable drinks and a friendly atmosphere. Recommended: Whiskey on the rocks. Starting price: $7.00 per drink.
- **The Library (East Village):** The Library is a cozy neighborhood bar offering daily drink specials, including discounted beers and cocktails. Recommended: Happy hour beer specials. Starting price: Varies by day and drink selection.
- **Boilermaker (East Village):** Boilermaker offers a selection of craft beers and shot combinations at affordable prices. Recommended: Beer and shot combo. Starting price: $10.00 for a beer and shot.
- **Billymark's West (Chelsea):** Billymark's West is a no-frills neighborhood bar with cheap drinks and a laid-back vibe. Recommended: Domestic beer. Starting price: $4.00 per beer.

Brooklyn:

- **Skinny Dennis (Williamsburg):** Skinny Dennis is a honky-tonk bar known for its cheap drinks and live music. Recommended: Frozen margarita. Starting price: $6.00 per drink.

- **The Turkey's Nest (Williamsburg)**: The Turkey's Nest serves up giant frozen margaritas in to-go cups at budget-friendly prices. Recommended: Frozen margarita. Starting price: $8.00 for a large.
- **The Charleston (Williamsburg)**: The Charleston offers daily drink specials, including discounted beers and cocktails, in a relaxed setting. Recommended: Happy hour specials. Starting price: Varies by day and drink selection.
- **Rocka Rolla (Williamsburg)**: Rocka Rolla is a rock 'n' roll-themed bar with affordable drinks and a laid-back atmosphere. Recommended: Beer and shot combo. Starting price: $8.00 for a beer and shot.
- **Lucky Dog (Williamsburg)**: Lucky Dog is a dive bar with a backyard patio and cheap drinks, including beer and cocktails. Recommended: Domestic beer. Starting price: $3.00 per beer.

Queens:

- **Albatross Bar (Astoria)**: Albatross Bar is a popular LGBTQ+ bar offering daily drink specials and a fun atmosphere. Recommended: Well drinks. Starting price: $6.00 per drink.
- **Break Bar & Billiards (Astoria)**: Break Bar & Billiards offers happy hour specials and a variety of beers on tap at affordable prices. Recommended: Happy hour beer specials. Starting price: Varies by day and drink selection.
- **Dutch Kills Bar (Long Island City)**: Dutch Kills Bar is a craft cocktail bar with a speakeasy vibe and reasonable prices. Recommended: Classic cocktail. Starting price: $10.00 per drink.
- **The Astoria Tavern (Astoria)**: The Astoria Tavern is a neighborhood bar with cheap drinks and a friendly

atmosphere. Recommended: Domestic beer. Starting price: $4.00 per beer.

- **The Bonnie (Astoria)**: The Bonnie offers a selection of beers, wines, and cocktails at affordable prices in a stylish setting. Recommended: House cocktail. Starting price: $10.00 per drink.

The Bronx:

- **Bronx Alehouse (Kingsbridge)**: Bronx Alehouse offers a rotating selection of craft beers and daily drink specials. Recommended: Craft beer on tap. Starting price: Varies by beer selection.
- **The Bronx Beer Hall (Arthur Avenue)**: The Bronx Beer Hall serves up a variety of local and craft beers in a lively market setting. Recommended: Local beer flight. Starting price: $10.00 for a flight.
- **Charlie's Bar & Kitchen (Mott Haven)**: Charlie's Bar & Kitchen offers happy hour specials and a selection of beers, wines, and cocktails at affordable prices. Recommended: Happy hour beer specials. Starting price: Varies by day and drink selection.
- **The Bronx Public (Mott Haven)**: The Bronx Public offers a diverse drink menu, including cocktails, wines, and beers, in a casual setting. Recommended: House cocktail. Starting price: $10.00 per drink.
- **Bricks & Hops Beer Garden (Melrose)**: Bricks & Hops Beer Garden offers a variety of craft beers on tap and outdoor seating. Recommended: Craft beer flight. Starting price: $12.00 for a flight.

INSIDER TIP

PDT (Please Don't Tell) is a tiny speakeasy concealed behind a hot-dog joint. You need reservations to visit this secret bar. If it's your first time, try to avoid booking your reservation when the bar opens so that you can experience the entrance on your own. You enter through the phone booth.

INSIDER HISTORICAL INSIGHT
If you're into history pay a visit to Fraunces Tavern on Pearl Street. You can Study a lock of George Washington's hair — and his tooth — at Fraunces Tavern. A renovated historic tavern with a George Washington link offering pub eats & live music on weekends.

Here are some more of the cheapest speakeasies in NYC, sorted by borough:

Manhattan:

- The Back Room (Lower East Side): Tucked away behind an unmarked door and down a flight of stairs, The Back Room offers Prohibition-era vibes with reasonably priced drinks served in teacups and beer bottles disguised in paper bags.
- Bathtub Gin (Chelsea): Accessible through a coffee shop entrance, Bathtub Gin serves up classic cocktails in a cozy, vintage-inspired setting. While prices can vary, happy hour deals can offer some savings.

Brooklyn:

- Sunshine Laundromat (Greenpoint): This speakeasy hidden behind a functioning laundromat offers a quirky setting with pinball machines and affordable drink options, making it a favorite among locals.
- The Richardson (Williamsburg): With a laid-back atmosphere and reasonably priced cocktails, The Richardson provides a relaxed speakeasy experience without the upscale price tags.
- Little Branch (Gowanus): While not technically a speakeasy, Little Branch offers a cozy, dimly lit am-

biance reminiscent of Prohibition-era bars with affordable cocktails made by skilled bartenders.
Queens:

- Dutch Kills (Long Island City): Known for its classic cocktails and speakeasy ambiance, Dutch Kills offers reasonably priced drinks and a friendly atmosphere without the pretentiousness often associated with upscale bars.
- The Last Word (Astoria): This hidden gem in Astoria offers an intimate speakeasy experience with a diverse cocktail menu and affordable prices, making it a favorite among locals looking for a relaxed night out.

Clubs

When it comes to experiencing New York City's vibrant nightlife, there's no shortage of options to explore. From exclusive clubs to chic lounges, the city's nightlife scene offers something for everyone. However, navigating this bustling scene can be daunting, especially for those looking to enjoy a VIP experience without breaking the bank. Fortunately, with a bit of savvy and strategic planning, it's possible to enjoy the city's nightlife like a VIP on a budget.

One of the best ways to gain access to exclusive clubs and lounges in New York City is by signing up for guest lists or downloading apps that offer free or discounted entry. Many clubs and venues partner with these apps to attract patrons and fill their venues, making it easier for guests to gain entry without paying full price.

Signing up for guest lists or downloading these apps is typically free and straightforward. Simply provide your name, email address, and sometimes a phone number to receive notifications about upcoming events and special promotions. Some apps even offer perks like complimentary drinks or VIP table reservations for those who sign up.

Once you're on the guest list or have downloaded the app, you'll receive notifications about upcoming events and promotions. It's important to keep an eye on these notifications and RSVP in advance to secure your spot, as entry may be limited and first-come, first-served.

Arriving early can also sometimes result in waived cover charges or expedited entry, especially if you're on the guest list. Many clubs and lounges have a designated window of time when entry is free or discounted for those who arrive early, so arriving promptly can help you save money and avoid long lines.

In addition to signing up for guest lists and downloading apps, another tip for enjoying VIP nightlife experiences on a budget is to do your research and choose venues wisely. Look for venues that offer a good value for your money, such as those with affordable drink prices or special promotions like open bar hours.

Consider exploring neighborhoods outside of the traditional nightlife hotspots, such as Williamsburg in Brooklyn or Long Island City in Queens. These areas often have hidden gems and up-and-coming venues that offer a more laid-back atmosphere and lower prices compared to their Manhattan counterparts.

Finally, don't forget to dress to impress! Many exclusive clubs and lounges have strict dress codes, so be sure to dress appropriately for the venue you're planning to visit. This may mean wearing upscale attire like cocktail dresses or button-down shirts, and avoiding casual attire like sneakers or flip-flops.

Is the tap water drinkable?

Yes.

How much can you save haggling here?

Gentle haggling is common at markets in NYC. Haggling in stores is generally unacceptable, although some good-humoured bargaining at smaller artisan or craft shops is cool if you are making multiple purchases.

Enjoy your first Day for under $20

Start early by visiting the American Museum of Natural History for free. Then great a cheap bagel and coffee and take a couple of hours to explore Central Park. Enjoy highlights such as Strawberry Fields, Sheeps Meadow, the Bow Bridge and the Bethesda Fountain. Follow the aromas to one of the numerous delis on 7th Ave. Explore Midtown Manhattan, visiting Times Square, Fifth Avenue, the Madison Square Garden and much more. Take the 1 train from Times Square to South Ferry. Jump on board the Staten Island ferry for unforgettable views of the Statue of Liberty. Take the 1 train back up to Christopher St/Sheridan Square. Get take away pizza in 'Bleecker St Pizza' both in the West Village. Wander down Bleecker Street until you come to MacDougal St - the heart of Greenwich Village. Go for a beer in one of the many bars before heading home to sleep.

What you need to Need to Know before you go

Currency: Dollar
Language: English
Money: Widely available ATMs.
Visas: The US Visa Waiver Program allows nationals of 38 countries to enter the US without a visa, but
you must fill out an ESTA application before departing.
http://www.doyouneedvisa.com/
Time: GMT - 5
When to Go
High Season: July and August.
Shoulder: May, April, June
Low Season: September to May.
Important Numbers
113 Ambulance
112 Police

Getting out of New York cheaply

Buses:

Megabus: Megabus offers budget-friendly bus services from NYC to various destinations in neighboring states and beyond. Prices can start as low as $1 for early bookings, but typically range from $10 to $50 depending on the destination and time of booking. Buses depart from the Port Authority Bus Terminal in Manhattan.

Greyhound: Greyhound also provides affordable bus services from NYC to cities across the United States. Fares vary based on the destination and time of travel but generally range from $20 to $100. Greyhound buses depart from the Port Authority Bus Terminal as well.

BoltBus: BoltBus is another option for inexpensive travel, with fares often starting at $1 for early bookings. Prices can range from $10 to $50 depending on the destination and time of booking. BoltBus operates from various locations in NYC, including Midtown Manhattan and Chinatown.

Amtrak:

Northeast Regional: Amtrak's Northeast Regional service connects NYC with major cities along the East Coast, such as Boston, Philadelphia, and Washington, D.C. Fares can vary widely based on the destination, time of booking, and class of service. Prices typically range from $30 to $200 or more for one-way tickets.

Acela Express: For faster travel between NYC and cities like Boston and Washington, D.C., consider Amtrak's Acela Express service. While pricier than the Northeast Regional, fares start around $80 and can go up to $400 or more for business class.

Long-Distance Trains: Amtrak also operates long-distance trains from NYC to destinations across the country, including Chicago, Miami, and New Orleans. Prices vary significantly depending on the route, time of booking, and class of service, with fares starting from $50 and going up to several hundred dollars or more for sleeper accommodations.

Flights:

Budget Airlines: Several budget airlines like Spirit Airlines, Frontier Airlines, and JetBlue offer cheap flights from NYC to domestic destinations. Prices can be as low as $50 for one-way tickets, especially if booked well in advance or during promotions.

Flight Comparison Websites: Utilize flight comparison websites like Skyscanner, Google Flights, or Kayak to find the cheapest fares from NYC airports (JFK, LaGuardia, Newark). Be flexible with travel dates and consider flying midweek or during off-peak hours for the best deals.

Alternative Airports: Consider flying out of alternative airports like Stewart International Airport (SWF) or Trenton-Mercer Airport (TTN) for potentially lower fares. These airports may have fewer flight options but can offer significant savings, especially for budget-conscious travelers.

Airport Lounges:

Priority Pass: If you have Priority Pass membership, you can access airport lounges worldwide, including those at NYC airports. Membership plans vary in price, but some credit cards offer complimentary Priority Pass membership as a benefit.

Credit Card Lounges: Certain credit cards, such as the Chase Sapphire Reserve or American Express Platinum, offer access to airport lounges as part of their benefits. Check your credit card's terms and conditions to see if you're eligible for lounge access and which lounges you can visit.

Day Passes: Some airport lounges offer day passes for purchase, allowing travelers to access amenities like comfortable seating, complimentary snacks, and beverages for a fee. Prices for day passes typically range from $30 to $50, depending on the lounge and airport.

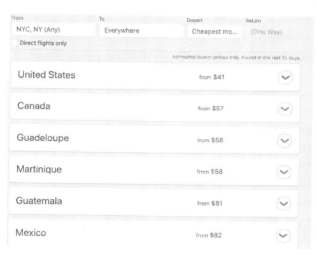

Avoid these tourist traps or scams

Avoiding tourist traps and scams is essential for any traveler looking to protect their budget and have a smooth experience in NYC. Unfortunately, scams are prevalent, especially near popular attractions. Here are some tips to steer clear of common pitfalls:

- **Beware of Fake Ticket Sellers:** One notorious scam involves individuals selling fake tickets to access Liberty Island, home of the Statue of Liberty. To avoid falling victim to these scams, only purchase tickets from the official provider, Statue Cruises. Buying tickets online in advance is the safest option to ensure authenticity and avoid being conned by seemingly legitimate salespeople who may approach you near tourist sites.
- **Stay Vigilant Against Scammers:** If approached by someone suspicious, it's wise to employ a simple tactic like saying "sorry, no English" and swiftly moving on. Be wary of overly friendly strangers offering deals or assistance, especially near tourist hotspots.
- **Exercise Caution on Public Transportation:** While the local subway system is an efficient way to navigate the city, be mindful that some routes may take longer than expected. Research your journey in advance and consider alternative transportation options if time is a concern. Additionally, be cautious of crowded subway cars and keep an eye on your belongings to prevent grab-and-run thefts.
- **Respect Local Customs and Etiquette:** Avoid causing disruptions or inconvenience to locals by refraining from stopping abruptly on sidewalks to take

photos. This behavior can be frustrating for New Yorkers trying to navigate busy streets. Instead, find a less crowded area or step to the side to capture your shots.

- **Stay Informed and Alert:** Stay updated on common scams and safety tips by consulting reliable travel resources and local authorities. Remain vigilant in crowded areas, tourist attractions, and public transportation hubs, where pickpockets and scammers may target unsuspecting visitors.

Checklist of the top 20 things to do in NYC

- ☑ Statue of Liberty and Ellis Island
- ☑ Empire State Building Observatory
- ☑ Central Park
- ☑ Times Square
- ☑ Broadway Show
- ☑ Metropolitan Museum of Art
- ☑ 9/11 Memorial and Museum
- ☑ Brooklyn Bridge Walk
- ☑ High Line Park
- ☑ Museum of Modern Art (MoMA)
- ☑ Rockefeller Center and Top of the Rock
- ☑ Grand Central Terminal
- ☑ One World Observatory
- ☑ Statue of Liberty Cruise
- ☑ Brooklyn Botanic Garden
- ☑ The Bronx Zoo
- ☑ Chelsea Market
- ☑ United Nations Headquarters Tour
- ☑ Radio City Music Hall Tour
- ☑ New York Public Library

RECAP: Enjoy a $5,000 trip to New York for $350

Here's how to enjoy a $5,000 trip to New York for just $350:

Stay in East Williamsburg: Opt for accommodations outside of Manhattan in East Williamsburg. This neighborhood offers a safe and vibrant atmosphere, with plenty of shops and bars. Airbnb rooms can be found for as low as $30 a night, and it's conveniently located near the L line for easy access to Manhattan. Potential saving: $600.

Blind book hotels or use Priceline's express deals: Take advantage of blind booking options like Last Minute Top Secret hotels or Priceline's express deals to snag discounted rates on four-star hotels, sometimes as low as $60 a night.

Use Too Good To Go: Save on restaurant expenses by picking up "magic bags" for dinner through the Too Good To Go app. These bags contain surplus food from restaurants at a fraction of the price. Remember to bring a spork for convenience.

Restaurant deals and cheap Michelin star restaurants: Explore midday lunch menus or happy hour deals offered by many restaurants in NYC. Additionally, indulge in the city's renowned Michelin star restaurants by taking advantage of discounted menu options, saving potentially up to $2,000.

Have a picnic: Enjoy a budget-friendly meal by having a picnic in Sheep's Meadow in Central Park. Grab some pizza and beers and soak in the sun while experiencing a favorite local pastime.

Visit museums/attractions on free days: Plan your museum and gallery visits around their free or discounted admission days to save on attraction costs. With proper timing, you can experience cultural sites without spending much, potentially saving $250.

Get Broadway tickets super cheap: Score discounted Broadway tickets through various methods outlined earlier, saving up to $350 on premium theater experiences.

Enjoy incredible views from Roosevelt tram and ferries: Take the Roosevelt tram for stunning nighttime views of the city for just $6 round trip. Alternatively, opt for inexpensive ferry rides to enjoy scenic views of New York's skyline.

Get out cheaply: If you're planning to explore other cities in the States, consider booking affordable onward journeys with services like Megabus, with fares starting as low as $5.

By following these tips and tricks, you can enjoy the best of New York City without breaking the bank, making your $5,000 trip affordable at just $350.

Money Mistakes in New York

Cost	Impact	Solution	Note
Ignoring Daily Deals and Discounts	NYC is known for its vibrant cultural scene, with many museums, theaters, and attractions offering discounted admission on certain days or times.	Always check for special promotions, coupons, or online deals before purchasing tickets to save money.	
Using your home currency	Some credit card rates charge for every transaction in another currency. Check carefully before you use it	Use a prepaid currency card like Wise Multi-Currency Debit Card.	If you wouldn't borrow money from a friend or relative for your trip, don't borrow it from a credit card company.
Not using the subway	$33 for unlimited travel will enable you to go all over the city for an entire week. Taxi's would cost you hundreds and result in a lot of time lost to traffic.	Buy a Subway pass	Many tourists rely solely on taxis or ride-sharing services, which can quickly add up in costs.
Buying bottled water	At $1 a bottle, this is a cost that can mount up quickly	Refill from the tap. Bring an on the go water filter bottle like Water-to-go or use life-straw.	
Eating like a tourist	Eating at tourist traps can triple your bill. Choose wisely	Star cheap eats on google maps so you're never far from one	
Not visiting attractions during their free times	You can save $500 on entrance fees just going during the free times	Make an itinerary.	

What to remember	How to Save Money	Additional Tips
Accommodation	Look for deals on budget hotels or consider hostels. Airbnb outside Manhattan can be cheaper.	Staying in neighborhoods like Queens or Brooklyn can offer lower prices.
Transportation	Use public transportation with a MetroCard. Consider a 7-day unlimited pass if staying for a week.	Walking is not only free but lets you see more of the city.
Dining	Eat where locals do; explore ethnic neighborhoods for affordable meals. Avoid tourist traps.	Food trucks and markets offer delicious options at lower costs.
Sightseeing	Take advantage of free days at museums and free walking tours.	Parks, bridges, and landmarks like Times Square cost nothing to explore.
Entertainment	Look for discounted Broadway tickets through TKTS or rush tickets. Free events happen citywide.	Outdoor concerts and festivals are often free during the summer.
Shopping	Explore discount outlets and thrift stores. Sample sales can offer designer goods at a fraction of the cost.	Tax-free shopping on clothing and shoes under $110.
Operas and Performances	Utilize rush tickets and special offers like "Fridays Under 40" at the Metropolitan Opera.	Student discounts are available for those with a valid ID.
City Passes	Consider purchasing a tourist pass like the New York Pass or City-PASS for multiple attractions.	Evaluate if you'll visit enough attractions to make the pass worth the investment.

The secret to saving HUGE amounts of money when travel-ling to New York is...

Your mindset. Money is an emotional topic, if you associate words like cheapskate, Miser (and its £9.50 to go into Charles Dickens New York house, oh the Irony) with being thrifty when traveling you are likely to say 'F-it' and spend your money need-lessly because you associate pain with saving money. You pay now for an immediate reward. Our brains are prehistoric; they focus on surviving day to day. Travel companies and hotels know this and put trillions into making you believe you will be happier when you spend on their products or services. Our poor brains are up against outdated programming and an onslaught of adver-tisements bombarding us with the message: spending money on travel equals PLEASURE. To correct this carefully lodged propa-ganda in your frontal cortex, you need to imagine your future self.

Saving money does not make you a cheapskate. It makes you smart. How do people get rich? They invest their money. They don't go out and earn it; they let their money earn more money. So every time you want to spend money, imagine this: while you travel, your money is working for you, not you for money. While you sleep, the money, you've invested is going up and up. That's a pleasure a pricey entrance fee can't give you. Thinking about putting your money to work for you tricks your brain into believing you are not withholding pleasure from yourself, you are saving your money to invest so you can go to even more amazing places. You are thus turning thrifty travel into a pleasure fueled sport.

When you've got money invested - If you want to splash your cash on a first-class airplane seat - you can. I can't tell you how to invest your money, only that you should. Saving $20 on taxis doesn't seem like much, but over time you could save upwards of $15,000 a year, which is a deposit for a house which you can rent on Airbnb to finance more travel. Your brain making money looks like your brain on cocaine, so tell yourself saving money is making money.

Scientists have proved that imagining your future self is the easiest way to associate pleasure with saving money. You can download FaceApp — which will give you a picture of what you will look like older and grayer, or you can take a deep breath just before spending money and ask yourself if you will regret the purchase later.

The easiest ways to waste money traveling are:

Getting a taxi. The solution to this is to always download the google map before you go. Many taxi drivers will drive you around for 15 minutes when the place you were trying to get to is a 5-minute walk… remember while not getting an overpriced taxi to tell yourself, 'I am saving money to free myself for more travel.' Spending money on overpriced food when hungry. The solution: carry snacks. A banana and an apple will cost you, in most places, less than a dollar.

Spending on entrance fees to top-rated attractions. If you really want to do it, spend the money happily. If you're conflicted, sleep on it. I don't regret spending $200 on a sky dive over the Great Barrier Reef; I regret going to the top of the shard on a cloudy day in London for $60. Only you can know, but make sure it's your decision and not the marketing directors at said top-rated attraction.

Telling yourself 'you only have the chance to see/eat/experience it now'. While this might be true, make sure YOU WANT to spend the money. Money spent is money you can't invest, and often you can have the same experience for much less.

You can experience luxurious travel on a small budget, which will trick your brain into thinking you're already a high-roller, which will mean you'll be more likely to act like one and invest your money. Stay in five-star hotels for $5 by booking on the day of your stay on booking.com to enjoy last-minute deals. You can go to fancy restaurants using daily deal sites. Ask your airline about last-minute upgrades to first-class or business. I paid $100 extra on a $179 ticket to Cuba from Germany to be bumped to Business Class. When you ask, it will surprise you what you can get both at hotels and airlines.

Travel, as the saying goes, is the only thing you spend money on that makes you richer. You can easily waste money, making it difficult to enjoy that metaphysical wealth. The biggest money saving secret is to turn bargain hunting into a pleasurable activity, not an annoyance. Budgeting consciously can be fun, don't feel disappointed because you don't spend the $60 to go into an attraction. Feel good because soon that $60 will soon earn money for you. Meaning, you'll have the time and money to enjoy more metaphysical wealth while your bank balance increases.

So there it is. You can save a small fortune by being strategic with your trip planning. We've arranged everything in the guide to offer the best bang for your buck. Which means we took the view that if it's not an excellent investment for your money, we wouldn't include it. Why would a guide called 'Super Cheap' include lots of overpriced attractions? That said, if you think we've missed something or have unanswered questions, ping me an email: philgtang@gmail.com I'm on central Europe time and usually reply within 8 hours of getting your mail. We like to think of our guide books as evolving organisms helping our readers travel better cheaper. We use reader questions via email to update this book year round so you'll be helping other readers and yourself.

Don't put your dreams off!

Time is a currency you never get back and travel is its greatest return on investment. Plus, now you know you can visit New York for a fraction of the price most would have you believe.

View from Brooklyn Bridge

Thank you for reading

Dear **Lovely Reader**,

If you have found this book useful, please consider writing a quick review on Amazon.

One person from every 1000 readers leaves a review on Amazon. It would mean more than you could ever know if you were one of our 1 in 1000 people to take the time to write a brief review.

Thank you so much for reading again and for spending your time and investing your trips future in Super Cheap Insider Guides. One last note, please don't listen to anyone who says 'Oh no, you can't visit New York on a budget'. Unlike you, they didn't have this book. You can do ANYWHERE on a budget with the right insider advice and planning. Sure, learning to travel to New York on a budget that doesn't compromise on anything or drastically compromise on safety or comfort levels is a skill, but this guide has done the detective work for you. Now it is time for you to put the advice into action.

Phil and the Super Cheap Insider Guides Team

P.S If you need any more super cheap tips we'd love to hear from you e-mail me at philgtang@gmail.com, we have a lot of contacts in every region, so if there's a specific bargain you're hunting we can help you find it.

Your Next Travel Guide is on me

Simply leave an honest, verified purchase review on Amazon and choose your next guide for free! Email me a screenshot and the name of the book you want: philgtang@gmail.com

COUNTRY GUIDES

Super Cheap AUSTRALIA
Super Cheap Austria
Super Cheap BAHAMAS
Super Cheap BARBADOS
Super Cheap BERMUDA
Super Cheap BRAZIL
Super Cheap CANADA
Super Cheap DENMARK
Super Cheap Dominican Republic
Super Cheap FIJI
Super Cheap FINLAND
Super Cheap FRANCE
Super Cheap GRENADA
Super Cheap GERMANY
Super Cheap GREECE
Super Cheap ICELAND
Super Cheap ITALY
Super Cheap IRELAND
Super Cheap JAMAICA
Super Cheap JAPAN
Super Cheap LUXEMBOURG
Super Cheap MALAYSIA
Super Cheap MALDIVES
Super Cheap MEXICO

Super Cheap NETHERLANDS
Super Cheap NEW ZEALAND
Super Cheap NORWAY
Super Cheap Saint Martin/ Sint Maarten
Super Cheap SOUTH KOREA
Super Cheap SPAIN
Super Cheap SWITZERLAND
Super Cheap UAE
Super Cheap UNITED KINGDOM
Super Cheap UNITED STATES

CITIES / TOWNS

Super Cheap ADELAIDE
Super Cheap ALASKA
Super Cheap AUSTIN
Super Cheap BANFF
Super Cheap BANGKOK
Super Cheap BARCELONA
Super Cheap BELFAST
Super Cheap BERMUDA
Super Cheap BORA BORA
Super Cheap BRITISH VIRGIN ISLANDS
Super Cheap BUDAPEST
Super Cheap Great Barrier Reef
Super Cheap CAMBRIDGE
Super Cheap CANCUN
Super Cheap CHIANG MAI
Super Cheap CHICAGO
Super Cheap Copenhagen
Super Cheap DOHA
Super Cheap DUBAI
Super Cheap DUBLIN
Super Cheap EDINBURGH
Super Cheap GALWAY
Super Cheap Guadeloupe
Super Cheap HELSINKI
Super Cheap LIMA

Super Cheap LISBON
Super Cheap MALAGA
Super Cheap Martinique
Super Cheap Machu Pichu
Super Cheap MIAMI
Super Cheap Milan
Super Cheap Montpellier
Super Cheap NASHVILLE
Super Cheap NAPA
Super Cheap NEW ORLEANS
Super Cheap NEW YORK
Super Cheap PARIS
Super Cheap PRAGUE
Super Cheap SANTORINI
Super Cheap SEATTLE
Super Cheap St. Vincent and the Grenadines
Super Cheap SEYCHELLES
Super Cheap SINGAPORE
Super Cheap ST LUCIA
Super Cheap TORONTO
Super Cheap Turks and Caicos
Super Cheap VANCOUVER
Super Cheap VENICE
Super Cheap VIENNA
Super Cheap YOSEMITE
Super Cheap ZURICH
Super Cheap ZANZIBAR

Bonus Travel Hacks

I've included these bonus travel hacks to help you plan and enjoy your trip to New York cheaply, joyfully, and smoothly. Perhaps they will even inspire you to start or renew a passion for long-term travel.

Common pitfalls when it comes to al-locating money to **your desires** while traveling

Beware of Malleable mental accounting

Let's say you budgeted spending only $30 per day in New York but then you say well if I was at home I'd be spending $30 on food as an everyday purchase so you add another $30 to your budget. Don't fall into that trap as the likelihood is you still have expenses at home even if its just the cost of keeping your freezer going.

Beware of impulse purchases in New York

Restaurants that you haven't researched and just idle into can sometimes turn out to be great, but more often, they turn out to suck, especially if they are near tourist attrac-tions. Make yourself a travel itinerary including where you'll eat breakfast and lunch. Dinner is always more expensive, so the meal best to enjoy at home or as a takeaway. This book is full of incredible cheap eats. All you have to do is plan to go to them.

Social media and FOMO (Fear of Missing Out)

'The pull of seeing acquaintances spend money on travel can often be a more powerful motivator to spend more while traveling than seeing an advertisement.' Beware of what you allow to influence you and go back to the question, what's the best money I can spend today?

Now-or-never sales strategies

One reason tourists are targeted by salespeople is the success of the now-or-never strategy. If you don't spend the money now... your never get the opportunity again. Rarely is this true.

Instead of spending your money on something you might not actually desire, take five minutes. Ask yourself, do I really want this? And return to the answer in five minutes. Your body will either say an absolute yes with a warm, excited feeling or a no with a weak, obscure feeling.

Unexpected costs

"Holding on to anger is like grasping a hot coal with the intent of throwing it at someone else; you only hurt yourself." The Buddha.

One downside to traveling is unexpected costs. When these spring up from airlines, accommodation providers, tours and on and on, they feel like a punch in the gut. During the pandemic my earnings fell to 20% of what they are normally. No one was traveling, no one was buying travel guides. My accountant out of nowhere significantly raised his fee for the year despite the fact there was a lot less money to count. I was so angry I consulted a lawyer who told me you will spend more taking him to court than you will paying his bill. I had to get myself into a good feeling place before I paid his bill, so I googled how to feel good paying someone who has scammed you.

The answer: Write down that you will receive 10 times the amount you are paying from an unexpected source. I did that. Four months later, the accountant wrote to me. He had applied for a COVID subsidy for me and I would receive... you guessed it almost exactly 10 times his fee.

Make of that what you want. I don't wish to get embroiled in a conversation about what many term 'woo-woo', but the result of my writing that I would receive 10 times the amount made me feel much, much better when paying him. And ultimately, that was a gift in itself. So next time some airline or train operator or hotel/ Airbnb sticks you with an unexpected fee, immediately write that you will receive 10 times the amount you are paying from an unexpected source. Rise your vibe and skip the added price of feeling angry.

Hack your allocations for your New York Trip

"The best trick for saving is to eliminate the decision to save." Perry Wright of Duke University.

Put the money you plan to spend in New York on a pre-paid card in the local currency. This cuts out two problems - not knowing how much you've spent and totally avoiding expensive currency conversion fees.

You could even create separate spaces. This much for transportation, this for tours/entertainment, accommodation and food. We are reluctant to spend money that is pre-assigned to categories or uses.

Write that you want to enjoy a $3,000 trip for $500 to your New York trip. Countless research shows when you put goals in writing, you have a higher chance of following through.

Spend all the money you want to on buying experiences in New York

"Experiences are like good relatives that stay for a while and then leave. Objects are like relatives who move in and stay past their welcome." Daniel Gilbert, psychologist from Harvard University.

Economic and psychological research shows we are happier buying brief experiences on vacation rather than buying stuff to wear so give yourself freedom to spend on experiences knowing that the value you get back is many many times over.

Make saving money a game

There's one day a year where all the thrift shops where me and my family live sell everything there for a $1. My wife and I hold a contest where we take $5 and buy an entire outfit for each other. Whoever's outfit is liked more wins. We also look online to see whose outfit would have cost more to buy new. This year, my wife even snagged me an Armani coat for $1. I liked the coat when she showed it to me, but when I found out it was $500 new; I liked it and wore it a lot more.

Quadruple your money

Every-time you want to spend money, imagine it quadrupled. So the $10 you want to spend is actually $40. Now imagine that what you want to buy is four times the price. Do you still want it? If yes, go enjoy. If not, you've just saved yourself money, know you can choose to invest it in a way that quadruples or allocate it to something you really want to give you a greater return.

Understand what having unlimited amounts of money to spend in New York actually looks like

Let's look at what it would be like to have unlimited amounts of money to spend on your trip to New York.

Isolation

You take a private jet to your private New York hotel. There you are lavished with the best food, drink, and entertainment. Spending vast amounts of money on vacation equals being isolated.

If you're on your honeymoon and you want to be alone with your Amore, this is wonderful, but it can be equally wonderful to make new friends. Know this a study 'carried out by Brigham Young University, Utah found that while obesity increased risk of death by 30%, loneliness increased it by half.'

Comfort

Money can buy you late check outs of five-star hotels and priority boarding on airlines, all of which add up to comfort. But as this book has shown you, saving money in New York doesn't minimize comfort, that's just a lie travel agencies littered with glossy brochures want you to believe.

You can do late-check outs for free with the right credit cards and priority boarding can be purchased with a lot of airlines from $4. If you want to go big with first-class or business, flights offset your own travel costs by renting your own home or you can upgrade at the airport often for a fraction of what you would have paid booking a business flight online.

MORE TIPS TO FIND CHEAP FLIGHTS

"The use of travelling is to regulate imagination by reality, a nd instead of thinking how things may be, to see them as t hey are." Samuel Jackson

If you're working full-time, you can save yourself a lot of money by requesting your time off from work starting in the middle of the week. Tuesdays and Wednesdays are the cheapest days to fly. You can save thousands just by adjusting your time off.

The simplest secret to booking cheap flights is open parameters. Let's say you want to fly from Chicago to Paris. You enter the USA in from and select New York under to. You may find flights from New York City to Paris for $70. Then you just need to find a cheap flight to NYC. Make sure you calculate full costs, including if you need airport accommodation and of course getting to and from airports, **but in nearly every instance open parameters will save you at least half the cost of the flight.**

If you're not sure about where you want to go, use open parameters to show you the cheapest destinations from your city. Start with skyscanner.net they include the low-cost airlines that others like Kayak leave out. Google Flights can also show you cheap destinations. To see these leave the WHERE TO section blank. Open parameters can also show you the cheapest dates to fly. If you're flexible, you can save up to 80% of the flight cost. Always check the weather at your destination before you book. Sometimes a $400 flight will be $20, because it's monsoon season. But hey, if you like the rain, why not?

ALWAYS USE A PRIVATE BROWSER TO BOOK FLIGHTS

Skyscanner and other sites track your IP address and put prices up and down based on what they determine your strength of conviction to buy. e.g. if you've booked one-way and are looking for the return, these sites will jack the prices up by in most cases 50%. Incognito browsing pays.

Use a VPN such as Hola to book your flight from your destination

Install Hola, change your destination to the country you are flying to. The location from which a ticket is booked can affect the price significantly as algorithms consider local buying power.

Choose the right time to buy your ticket.

Choose the right time to buy your ticket, as purchasing tickets on a Sunday has been proven to be cheaper. If you can only book during the week, try to do it on a Tuesday.

Mistake fares

Email alerts from individual carriers are where you can find the best 'mistake fares". This is where a computer error has resulted in an airline offering the wrong fare. In my experience, it's best to sign up to individual carriers email lists, but if you ARE lazy Secret Flying puts together a daily roster of mistake fares. Visit https://www.secretflying.com/errorfare/ to see if there're any errors that can benefit you.

Fly late for cheaper prices

Red-eye flights, the ones that leave later in the day, are typically cheaper and less crowded, so aim to book that flight if possible. You will also get through the airport much quicker at the end of the day. Just make sure there's ground transport available for when you land. You don't want to save $50 on the airfare and spend it on a taxi to your accommodation.

Use this APP for same day flights

If your plans are flexible, use 'Get The Flight Out' (http://www.gtfoflights.com/) a fare tracker Hopper that shows you same-day deeply discounted flights. This is best for long-haul flights with major carriers. You can often find a British Airways round-trip from JFK Airport to Heathrow for $300. If you booked this in advance, you'd pay at least double.

Take an empty water bottle with you

Airport prices on food and drinks are sky high. It disgusts me to see some airports charging $10 for a bottle of water. ALWAYS take an empty water bottle with you. It's relatively unknown, but most airports have drinking water fountains past the security check. Just type in your airport name to wateratairports.com to locate the fountain. Then once you've passed security (because they don't allow you to take 100ml or more of liquids) you can freely refill your bottle with water.

Round-the-World (RTW) Tickets

It is always cheaper to book your flights using a DIY approach. First, you may decide you want to stay longer in one country, and a RTW will charge you a hefty fee for changing your flight. Secondly, it all depends on where and when you travel and as we have discussed, there are many ways to ensure you pay way less than $1,500 for a year of flights. If you're travelling long-haul, the best strategy is to buy a return ticket, say New York, to Bangkok and then take cheap flights or transport around Asia and even to Australia and beyond.

Cut your costs to and from airports

Don't you hate it when getting to and from the airport is more expensive than your flight! And this is true in so many cities, especially European ones. For some reason, Google often shows the most expensive options. Use Omio to compare the cheapest transport options and save on airport transfer costs.

Car sharing instead of taxis

Check if New York has car sharing at the airport. Often they'll be tons of cars parked at the airport that are half the price of taking a taxi into the city. In most instances, you register your driving licence on an app and scan the code on the car to get going.

Checking Bags

Sometimes you need to check bags. If you do, put an AirTag inside. That way, you'll be about to see when you land where your bag is. This saves you the nail biting wait at baggage claim. And if worse comes to worst, and you see your bag is actually in another city, you can calmly stroll over to customer services and show them where your bag is.

Is it cheaper and more convenient to send your bags ahead?

Before you check your bags, check if it's cheaper to send them ahead of you with sendmybag.com obviously if you're staying in an Airbnb, you'll need to ask the hosts permission or you can time them to arrive the day after you. Hotels are normally very amenable.

What Credit Card Gives The Best Air Miles?

You can slash the cost of flights just for spending on a piece of plastic.

LET'S TALK ABOUT DEBT

Before we go into the best cards for each country, let's first talk about debt. The US system offers the best and biggest rewards. Why? Because they rely on the fact that many people living in the US will not pay their cards in full and the card will earn the bank significant interest payments. Other countries have a very different attitude towards money, debt, and saving than Americans. Thus in Germany and Austria the offerings aren't as favourable as the UK, New York and Australia, where debt culture is more widely embraced. The takeaway here is this: **Only spend on one of these cards when you have set-up an automatic total monthly balance repayment. Don't let banks profit from your lizard brain!**

The best air-mile credit cards for those living in the UK

Amex Preferred Rewards Gold comes out top for those living in the UK for 2024.

Here are the benefits:

- 20,000-point bonus on £3,000 spend in first three months. These can be used towards flights with British Airways, Virgin Atlantic, Emirates and Etihad, and often

other rewards, such as hotel stays and car hire.
- 1 point per £1 spent
- 1 point = 1 airline point
- Two free visits a year to airport lounges
- No fee in year one, then £140/yr

The downside:

- Fail to repay fully and it's 59.9% rep APR interest, incl fee

You'll need to cancel before the £140/yr fee kicks in year two if you want to avoid it.

The best air-mile credit cards for those living in Canada

Aeroplan is the superior rewards program in Canada. The card has a high earn rate for Aeroplan Points, generating 1.5 points per $1 spent on eligible purchases. Look at the specifics of the eligible purchases https://www.aircanada.com/ca/en/aco/home/aeroplan/earn.html. If you're not spending on these things AMEX's Membership Rewards program offers you the best returns in Canada.

The best air-mile credit cards for those living in Germany

If you have a German bank account, you can apply for a Lufthansa credit card.

Earn 50,000 award miles if you spend $3,000 in purchases and paying the annual fee, both within the first 90 days.

Earn 2 award miles per $1 spent on ticket purchases directly from Miles & More integrated airline partners.

Earn 1 award mile per $1 spent on all other purchases.

The downsides

the €89 annual fee

Limited to fly with Lufthansa and its partners but you can capitalise on perks like the companion pass and airport lounge vouchers.

You need excellent credit to get this card.

The best air-mile credit cards for those living in Austria

"In Austria, Miles & More offers you a special credit card. You get miles for each purchase with the credit card. The Miles & More program calculates miles earned based on the distance flown and booking class. For European flights, the booking class is a flat rate. For intercontinental flights, mileage is calculated by multiplying the booking class by the distance flown." They offer a calculator so you can see how many points you could earn: https://www.miles-and-more.com/at/en/earn/airlines/mileage-calculator.html

The best air-mile credit cards for those living in Spain:

"The American Express card is the best known and oldest to earn miles, thanks to its membership Rewards program. When making payments with this card, points are added, which can then be exchanged for miles from airlines such as Iberia, Air Europa, Emirates or Alitalia." More information is available here: https://www.americanexpress.com/es-es/

The best air-mile credit cards for those living in Australia

ANZ Rewards Black comes out top for 2024.

180,000 bonus ANZ Reward Points (can get an $800 gift card) and $0 annual fee for the first year with the ANZ Rewards Black
Points Per Spend: 1 Velocity point on purchases of up to

$5,000 per statement period and 0.5 Velocity points there-after.
Annual Fee: $0 in the first year, then $375 after.
Ns no set minimum income required, however, there is a minimum credit limit of $15,000 on this card.

Here are some ways you can hack points onto this card: https://www.pointhacks.com.au/credit-cards/anz-rewards-black-guide/

The best air-mile credit card solution for those living in the USA with a POOR credit score

The downside to Airline Mile cards is that they require good or excellent credit scores, meaning 690 or higher.

If you have bad credit and want to use credit card air lines you will need to rebuild your credit poor. The Credit One Bank® Platinum Visa® for Rebuilding Credit is a good credit card for people with bad credit who don't want to place a deposit on a secured card. The Credit One Platinum Visa offers a $300 credit limit, rewards, and the potential for credit-limit increases, which in time will help rebuild your score.

PLEASE don't sign-up for any of these cards if you can't trust yourself to repay it in full monthly. This will only lead to stress for you.

In the USA, the Chase Sapphire Preferred card offers 60,000 bonus points after spending $4,000 in the first 3 months. Points transfer 1:1 to leading airline and hotel loyalty programs. However, it comes with a $95 annual fee, and after the first year, this fee remains. Additionally, there's a higher minimum spend requirement for bonus points and limited travel redemption options compared to premium cards. It requires a good credit score.

In the UK, the Amex Preferred Rewards Gold card provides a 20,000-point bonus on £3,000 spend in the first 3 months and earns 1 point per £1 spent. Cardholders also receive two free visits per year to airport lounges. While there's no fee in the first year, there's a £140 annual fee afterward. Drawbacks include a high 59.9% representative APR interest rate if the balance isn't repaid in full and limited acceptance compared to Visa/Mastercard. It also requires a good credit score.

For Australians, the ANZ Rewards Black card offers 180,000 bonus ANZ Reward Points and $0 annual fee for the first year. It earns 1 Velocity point on purchases up to $5,000 per statement period and has no set minimum income required. However, after the first year, there's a $375 annual fee, and rewards on purchases over $5,000 per statement period are limited. Moreover, there are limited airline partnerships compared to other cards. It also requires a good credit score.

In Canada, the American Express Gold Rewards Card grants 25,000 Membership Rewards points after spending $1,500 in the first 3 months and a $100 annual travel credit. It offers flexible redemption options including travel, merchandise, and gift cards. Nevertheless, there's a $150 annual fee and limited acceptance compared to Visa/Mastercard. Additionally, it has a higher minimum spend requirement compared to some other cards. It requires a good credit score.

In Germany, the Lufthansa Miles & More Credit Card offers 50,000 award miles upon spending $3,000 within the first 90 days. Cardholders earn 2 award miles per $1 spent on ticket purchases from Miles & More integrated partners. However, it comes with an €89 annual fee and is limited to flights with Lufthansa and its partners. Additionally, it requires excellent credit.

For Austria, the Miles & More Credit Card allows users to earn miles for each purchase and redeem them for flights based on distance flown and booking class. It also offers a mileage calculator for estimating points. However, it's limited to the Miles & More program, and there may be annual fees and other charges. Furthermore, it may have limited acceptance compared to other cards. Similar to Germany, it requires a good credit score.

In Switzerland, the SWISS Miles & More Credit Card allows cardholders to earn miles for every purchase and provides priority boarding and check-in with SWISS. Additionally, it has no foreign transaction fees. Nevertheless, it's also limited to the Miles & More program and may have annual fees and other charges. Furthermore, its acceptance may be limited compared to other cards. Like the other mentioned cards, it requires a good credit score.

Frequent Flyer Memberships

"Points" and "miles" are often used interchangeably, but they're usually two very different things. Maximise and diversify your rewards by utilising both.

A frequent-flyer program (FFP) is a loyalty program offered by an airline. They are designed to encourage airline customers to fly more to accumulate points (also called miles, kilometres, or segments) which can be redeemed for air travel or other rewards.

You can sign up with any FFP program for free. There are three major airline alliances in the world: Oneworld, SkyTeam and Star Alliance. I am with One World https://www.oneworld.com/members because the points can be accrued and used for most flights.

The best return on your points is to use them for international business or first class flights with lie-flat seats. You would need 3 times more miles compared to an economy flight, but if you paid cash, you'd pay 5 - 10 times more than the cost of the economy flight, so it really pays to use your points only for upgrades. The worst value for your miles is to buy an economy seat or worse, a gift from the airlines gift-shop.

Sign up for a family/household account to pool miles together. If you share a common address, you can claim the miles with most airlines. You can use AwardWallet to keep track of your miles. Remember that they only last for 2 years, so use them before they expire.

Delta Air Lines' SkyMiles program offers no blackout dates for award flights and the ability to earn miles through flights, credit card spending, and partners. However, it has variable award pricing, limited availability of saver-level award seats, and a miles expiration policy.

American Airlines' AAdvantage program boasts an extensive network of routes and partners. Elite status perks include complimentary upgrades, priority boarding, and waived fees. Nevertheless, it has dynamic award pricing, limited availability of saver-level award seats, and some benefits restricted to elite members.

United Airlines' MileagePlus program provides a wide range of redemption options including flights, upgrades, and merchandise. Its Star Alliance membership offers access to a global network. Yet, it has variable award pricing, limited availability of saver-level award seats, and some elite benefits restricted to higher-tier members.

Southwest Airlines' Rapid Rewards program stands out with no blackout dates or seat restrictions on award flights. Additionally, its Companion Pass program allows a designated companion to fly for free (excluding taxes and fees). However, its points value can vary depending on fare class, and it has limited international routes compared to other carriers.

British Airways' Executive Club allows Avios points to be redeemed for flights, upgrades, and partner awards. Tiered membership offers benefits like lounge access and priority check-in. Nonetheless, it has high fuel surcharges on some award flights, a distance-based award chart that may not offer good value for short-haul flights, and limited partner availability.

Emirates' Skywards program offers access to luxury experiences like first-class flights and premium lounges. Its family membership allows pooling of miles for faster rewards. However, it has high fuel surcharges on some award flights, limited availability of premium cabin award seats, and tier-based earning and benefits.

How to get 70% off a Cruise

An average cruise can set you back $4,000. If you dream of cruising the oceans, but find the pricing too high, look at repositioning cruises. You can save as much as 70% by taking a cruise which takes the boat back to its home port.

These one-way itineraries take place during low cruise seasons when ships have to reposition themselves to locations where there's warmer weather.

To find a repositioning cruise, go to vacationstogo.com/repositioning_cruises.cfm. This simple and often overlooked booking trick is great for avoiding long flights with children and can save you so much money!

It's worth noting we don't have any affiliations with any travel service or provider. The links we suggest are chosen based on our experience of finding the best deals.

Royal Caribbean offers repositioning cruises between continents, such as transatlantic or transpacific voyages. Passengers have the opportunity to explore multiple destinations during one cruise, typically with longer itineraries and more sea days. There's potential for lower fares compared to traditional cruises due to one-way routes. However, availability is limited as repositioning cruises are seasonal and occur during specific times of the year. Additionally, some passengers may prefer shorter, port-intensive itineraries, and it may involve one-way airfare or additional travel arrangements.

Princess Cruises provides repositioning cruises spanning various regions, including Asia, Europe, and the Americas.

They offer diverse itineraries with stops in different countries and regions, allowing for more onboard activities and relaxation. There's potential for lower fares compared to regular sailings. However, departure dates and availability are limited as repositioning cruises typically occur during shoulder seasons. Moreover, one-way itineraries may require additional travel arrangements.

Celebrity Cruises offers transatlantic and transpacific repositioning cruises between Europe, the Caribbean, and Alaska. They provide a modern luxury experience with upscale amenities and dining options, along with the opportunity to visit multiple destinations in one trip. However, availability is limited as repositioning cruises are seasonal and occur during specific times of the year. Additionally, higher fares for premium amenities and services may not fit all budgets, and there may be additional costs associated with one-way travel.

Holland America offers transatlantic and transpacific repositioning cruises, including itineraries between Europe, the Caribbean, and Alaska.

Relaxing at the Airport

The best way to relax at the airport is in a lounge where they provide free food, drinks, comfortable chairs, luxurious amenities (many have showers) and, if you're lucky, a peaceful ambience. If you're there for a longer time, look for Airport Cubicles, sleep pods which charge by the hour.

You can use your FFP Card (Frequent Flyer Memberships) to get into select lounges for free. Check your eligibility before you pay.

If you're travelling a lot, I'd recommend investing in a Priority Pass for the airport.

It includes 850-plus airport lounges around the world. The cost is $99 for the year and $27 per lounge visit or you can pay $399 for the year all inclusive.

If you need a lounge for a one-off day, you can get a Day Pass. Buy it online for a discount, it always works out cheaper than buying at the airport. Use www.LoungePass.com.

Lounges are also great if you're travelling with kids, as they're normally free for kids and will definitely cost you less than snacks for your little ones. The rule is that kids should be seen and not heard, so consider this before taking an overly excited child who wants to run around, or you might be asked to leave even after you've paid.

Priority Pass offers access to a large network of airport lounges worldwide, with various membership levels available. Some plans include free visits, but there's an annual membership fee and an additional fee for guest visits. Moreover, it's limited to participating lounges.

Credit cards provide complimentary lounge access as a card benefit, along with additional travel perks. There's no need for a separate membership, but premium cards often come with high annual fees. Additionally, lounge access is limited to specific lounges and may require minimum spending or qualifications.

Airline status grants lounge access based on frequent flyer status, available to elite members of airline loyalty programs. However, it requires achieving and maintaining elite status and is limited to specific airlines and alliances.

Day passes offer flexibility to purchase access only when needed, with no annual commitment. However, they can be expensive for frequent travelers, and availability may be limited depending on lounge capacity and policies.

Membership programs provide consistent lounge access with annual membership, along with loyalty benefits with the airline. Access to additional perks depends on the program, but there's an annual membership fee and it's limited to lounges operated by the airline or its partners.

Subscription services offer pay-per-visit access with no annual commitment and access to a variety of lounges. However, the per-visit fee may add up for frequent travelers, availability may be limited in some airports, and there may be additional fees for certain features or lounges.

How to spend money

Bank ATM fees vary from $2.50 per transaction to as high as $5 or more, depending on the ATM and the country. You can completely skip those fees by paying with card and using a card which can hold multiple currencies.

Budget travel hacking begins with a strategy to spend without fees. Your individual strategy depends on the country you legally reside in as to what cards are available. Happily there are some fin-tech solutions which can save you thousands on those pesky ATM withdrawal fees and are widely available globally. Here are a selection of cards you can pre-charge with currency for New York:

N26

N26 is a 12-year-old digital bank. I have been using them for over 6 years. The key advantage is fee-free card transactions abroad. They have a very elegant app, where you can check your timeline for all transactions listed in real time or manage your in-app security anywhere. The card you receive is a Mastercard so you can use it everywhere. If you lose the card, you don't have to call anyone, just open the app and swipe 'lock card'. It puts your purchases into a graph automatically so you can see what you spend on. You can open an account from abroad entirely online, all you need is your passport and a camera n26.com

Revolut

Revolut is a multi-currency account that allows you to hold and exchange 29 currencies and spend fee-free abroad. It's a UK based neobank, but accepts customers from all over the world.

Wise debit card

If you're going to be in one place for a long time, the Wise debit card is like having your travel money on a card – it lets you spend money at the real exchange rate.

Monzo

Monzo is good if your UK based. They offer a fee-free UK account. Fee-free international money transfers and fee-free spending abroad.

The downside

The cards above are debit cards, meaning you need to have money in those accounts to spend it. This comes with one big downside: safety. Credit card issuers' have "zero liability" meaning you're not liable for unauthorised charges. All the cards listed above do provide cover for unauthorised charges but times vary greatly in how quickly you'd get your money back if it were stolen.

The best option is to check in your country to see which credit cards are the best for travelling and set up monthly payments to repay the whole amount so you don't pay unnecessary interest. In the USA, Schwab regularly ranks at the top for travel credit cards. Credit cards are always the safer option when abroad simply because you get your money back faster if its stolen and if you're renting cars, most will give you free insurance when you book the car rental using the card, saving you money.

Always withdraw money; never exchange.

Money exchanges, whether they be on the streets or in the airports will NEVER give you a good exchange rate. Do not bring bundles of cash. Instead, withdraw local currency from the ATM as needed and try to use only free ATMs. Many in airports charge you a fee to withdraw cash. Look for bigger ATMs attached to banks to avoid this.

Recap

- Take cash from local, non-charging ATMs for the best rates.

- Never change at airport exchange desks unless you absolutely have to, then just change just enough to be able get to a bank ATM.

- Bring a spare credit card for emergencies.

- Split cash in various places on your person (pockets, shoes) and in your luggage. It's never sensible to keep your cash or cards all in one place.

- In higher risk areas, use a money belt under your clothes or put $50 in your shoe or bra.

Revolut

Revolut is a multi-currency account that allows you to hold and exchange 29 currencies and spend fee-free abroad. It's a UK based neobank, but accepts customers from all over the world.

Wise debit card

If you're going to be in one place for a long time the Wise debit card is like having your travel money on a card – it lets you spend money at the real exchange rate.

Monzo

Monzo is good if your UK based. They offer a fee-free UK account. Fee-free international money transfers and fee-free spending abroad.

The downside

The cards above are debit cards, meaning you need to have money in those accounts to spend it. This comes with one big downside: safety. Credit card issuers' have "zero liability" meaning you're not liable for unauthorised charges. All of the cards listed above do provide cover for unauthorised charges but times vary greatly in how quickly you'd get your money back if it were stolen.

The best option is to check in your country to see which credit cards are the best for travelling and set up monthly payments to repay the whole amount so you don't pay unnecessary interest. In the USA, Schwab[2] regularly ranks at the top for travel credit cards. Credit cards are always the safer option when abroad simply because you get your

------

[2] Charles Schwab High Yield Checking accounts refund every single ATM fee worldwide, require no minimum balance and have no monthly fee.

money back faster if its stolen and if you're renting cars, most will give you free insurance when you book the car rental using the card, saving you money.

Always withdraw money; never exchange.

Money exchanges whether they be on the streets or in the airports will NEVER give you a good exchange rate. Do not bring bundles of cash. Instead withdraw local currency from the ATM as needed and try to use only free ATM's. Many in airports charge you a fee to withdraw cash. Look for bigger ATM's attached to banks to avoid this.

Recap

- Take cash from local, non-charging ATMs for the best rates.
- Never change at airport exchange desks unless you ab-solutely have to, then just change just enough to be able get to a bank ATM.
- Bring a spare credit card for emergencies.
- Split cash in various places on your person (pockets, shoes) and in your luggage. Its never sensible to keep your cash or cards all in one place.
- In higher risk areas, use a money belt under your clothes or put $50 in your shoe or bra.

How NOT to be ripped off

"One of the great things about travel is that you find out how many good, kind people there are."
— Edith Wharton

The quote above may seem ill placed in a chapter entitled how not to be ripped off, but I included it to remind you that the vast majority of people do not want to rip you off. In fact, scammers are normally limited to three situations:

1. Around heavily visited attractions - these places are targeted purposively due to sheer footfall. Many criminals believe ripping people off is simply a numbers game.

2. In cities or countries with low-salaries or communist ideologies. If they can't make money in the country, they seek to scam foreigners. If you have travelled to India, Morocco or Cuba you will have observed this phenomenon.

3. When you are stuck and the person helping you know you have limited options.

Scammers know that most people will avoid confrontation. Don't feel bad about utterly ignoring someone and saying no. Here are six strategies to avoid being ripped off:

1. **Never ever agree to pay as much as you want. Always decide on a price before.**

Whoever you're dealing with is trained to tell you, they are uninterested in money. This is a trap. If you let people do this they will ask for MUCH MORE money at the end, and because you have used there service, you will feel obliged to pay. This is a conman's trick and nothing more.

2. Pack light

You can move faster and easier. If you take heavy luggage, you will end up taking taxis which are comparatively very costly over time.

3. NEVER use the airport taxi service. Plan to use public transport before you reach the airport.

4. Don't buy a sim card from the airport. Buy from the local supermarkets it will cost 50% less.

5. Eat at local restaurants serving regional food

Food defines culture. Exploring all delights available to the palate doesn't need to cost enormous sums.

6. **Ask the locals what something should cost,** and try not to pay over that.

7. **If you find yourself with limited options.** e.g. your taxi dumps you on the side of the road because you refuse to pay more (common in India and parts of South America) don't act desperate and negotiate as if you have other options or you will be extorted.

8. Don't blindly rely on social media[3]

Let's say you post in a Facebook group that you want tips for travelling to The Maldives. A lot of the comments you

[3] https://arstechnica.com/tech-policy/2019/12/social-media-platforms-leave-95-of-reported-fake-accounts-up-study-finds/

will receive come from guides, hosts and restaurants doing their own promotion. It's estimated that 50% or more of Facebook's current monthly active users are fake. And what's worse, a recent study found Social media platforms leave 95% of reported fake accounts up. These accounts are the digital versions of the men who hang around the Grand Palace in Bangkok telling tourists its closed, to divert you to shops where they will receive a commission for bringing you.

It can also be the case that genuine comments come from people who have totally different interests, beliefs and yes, budgets to yours. Make your experience your own and don't believe every comment you read.

Bottom line: use caution when accepting recommendations on social media and always fact-check with your own research.

Small tweaks on the road add up to big differences in your bank balance

Take advantage of other hotel amenities

If you fancy a swim but you're nowhere near the ocean, try the nearest hotel with a pool. As long as you buy a drink, the hotel staff will probably grant you access.

Fill up your mini bar for free.

Fill up your mini bar for free by storing things from the breakfast bar or grocery shop in your mini bar to give you a greater selection of drinks and food without the hefty price tag.

Save yourself some ironing

Use the steam from the shower to get rid of wrinkles in clothing. If something is creased, leave it trapped with the steam in the bathroom overnight for even better results.

See somewhere else for free

Opt for long stopovers, allowing you to experience another city without spending much money.

Wear your heaviest clothes

On the plane to save weight in your pack, allowing you to bring more with you. Big coats can then be used as pillows to make your flight more comfortable.

Don't get lost while you're away.

Find where you want to go using Google Maps, then type 'OK Maps' into the search bar to store this information for offline viewing.

Use car renting services

Share Now or Car2Go allow you to hire a car for 2 hours for $25 in a lot of European countries.

Share Rides

Use sites like blablacar.com to find others who are driving in your direction. It can be 80% cheaper than normal transport. Just check the drivers reviews.

Use free gym passes

Get a free gym day pass by googling the name of a local gym and free day pass.

When asked by people providing you a service where you are from..

If there's no price list for the service you are asking for, when asked where you are from, Say you are from a lesser-known poorer country. I normally say Macedonia, and if they don't know where it is, add it's a poor country. If you say UK, USA, the majority of Europe bar the well-known poorer countries taxi drivers, tour operators etc will match the price to what they think you pay at home.

Set-up a New Uber/ other car hailing app account for discounts

By googling you can find offers with $50 free for new users in most cities for Uber/ Lyft/ Bolt and alike. Just set up a new gmail.com email account to take advantage.

Where and How to Make Friends

"People don't take trips, trips take people." – John Stein-beck

Become popular at the airport

Want to become popular at the airport? Pack a power bar with multiple outlets and just see how many friends you can make. It's amazing how many people forget their chargers, or who packed them in the luggage that they checked in.

Stay in Hostels

First of all, Hostels don't have to be shared dorms, and they cater to a much wider demographic than is assumed. Hostels are a better environment for meeting people than hotels, and more importantly, they tended to open up excursion opportunities that further opened up that opportunity.

Or take up a hobby

If hostels are a definite no-no for you; find an interest. Take up a hobby where you will meet people. I've dived for years and the nature of diving is you're always paired up with a dive buddy. I met a lot of interesting people that way.

Small tweaks on the road add up to big differences in your bank balance

Take advantage of other hotel's amenities

If you fancy a swim but you're nowhere near the ocean, try the nearest hotel with a pool. As long as you buy a drink, the hotel staff will likely grant you access.

Fill up your mini bar for free.

Fill up your mini bar for free by storing things from the breakfast bar or grocery shop in your mini bar to give you a greater selection of drinks and food without the hefty price tag.

Save yourself some ironing

Use the steam from the shower to get rid of wrinkles in clothing. If something is creased, leave it trapped with the steam in the bathroom overnight for even better results.

See somewhere else for free

Opt for long stopovers, allowing you to experience another city without spending much money.

Wear your heaviest clothes

on the plane to save weight in your pack, allowing you to bring more with you. Big coats can then be used as pillows to make your flight more comfortable.

Don't get lost while you're away.

Find where you want to go using Google Maps, then type 'OK Maps' into the search bar to store this information for offline viewing.

Use car renting services

Share Now or Car2Go allow you to hire a car for 2 hours for $25 in a lot of Europe.

Share Rides

Use sites like blablacar.com to find others who are driving in your direction. It can be 80% cheaper than normal transport. Just check the drivers reviews.

Use free gym passes

Get a free gym day pass by googling the name of a local gym and free day pass.

When asked by people providing you a service where you are from..

If there's no price list for the service you are asking for, when asked where you are from, Say you are from a lesser-known poorer country. I normally say Macedonia, and if they don't know where it is, add it's a poor country. If you say UK, USA, the majority of Europe bar the well-known poorer countries taxi drivers, tour operators etc will match the price to what they think you pay at home.

Set-up a New Uber/ other car hailing app account for discounts

By googling you can find offers with $50 free for new users in most cities for Uber/ Lyft/ Bolt and alike. Just set up a new gmail.com email account to take advantage.

Where and How to Make Friends

"People don't take trips, trips take people." – John Stein-beck

Become popular at the airport

Want to become popular at the airport? Pack a power bar with multiple outlets and just see how many friends you can make. It's amazing how many people forget their chargers, or who packed them in the luggage that they checked in.

Stay in Hostels

First of all, Hostels don't have to be shared dorms, and they cater to a much wider demographic than is assumed. Hostels are a better environment for meeting people than hotels, and more importantly they tended to open up excursion opportunities that further opened up that opportunity.

Or take up a hobby

If hostels are a definite no-no for you; find an interest. Take up a hobby where you will meet people. I've dived for years and the nature of diving is you're always paired up with a dive buddy. I met a lot of interesting people that way.

When unpleasantries come your way...

We all have our good and bad days travelling, and on a bad day you can feel like just taking a flight home. Here are some ways to overcome common travel problems:

Anxiety when flying

It has been over 40 years since a plane has been brought down by turbulence. Repeat that number to yourself: 40 years! Planes are built to withstand lighting strikes, extreme storms and ultimately can adjust course to get out of their way. Landing and take-off are when the most accidents happen, but you have statistically three times the chance of winning a huge jackpot lottery, then you do of dying in a plane crash.

If you feel afraid on the flight, focus on your breathing saying the word 'smooth' over and over until the flight is smooth. Always check the airline safety record on airlinerating.com I was surprised to learn Ryanair and Easyjet as much less safe than Wizz Air according to those ratings because they sell similarly priced flights. If there is extreme turbulence, I feel much better knowing I'm in a 7 star safety plane.

Supplements can really help relieve the symptoms of anxiety. Here are the best. I've taken all of these and never have problems, but please consult a medical doctor if you are on any other medications.

Supplement: Magnesium Glycinate

Benefits: Tons of clinical data say it helps relax muscles and promote calmness.

Cons: May cause gastrointestinal discomfort in some individuals.

Supplement: CBD oil (Cannabidiol)

Benefits: May help reduce anxiety and promote relaxation.

Cons: Legality and regulations may vary by region.

Supplement: Valerian Root

Benefits: Herbal remedy for anxiety and sleep.

Cons: May cause drowsiness and dizziness.

Supplement: Chamomile
Benefits: Herbal tea with calming properties.
Cons: May cause allergic reactions in some individuals.

Wanting to sleep instead of seeing new places

This is a common problem. Just relax, there's little point doing fun things when you feel tired. Factor in jet-lag to your travel plans. When you're rested and alert you'll enjoy your new temporary home much more. Many people hate the first week of a long-trip because of jet-lag and often blame this on their first destination, but its rarely true. Ask travellers who 'hate' a particular place and you will see that very often they either had jet-lag or an unpleasant journey there.

Going over budget

Come back from a trip to a monster credit card bill? Hopefully, this guide has prevented you from returning to an unwanted bill. Of course, there are costs that can creep up and this is a reminder about how to prevent them making their way on to your credit card bill:

- To and from the airport. Solution: leave adequate time and take the cheapest method - book before.

- Baggage. Solution: take hand luggage and post things you might need to yourself.

- Eating out. Solution: go to cheap eats places and suggest those to friends.

- Parking. Solution: use apps to find free parking

- Tipping. Solution Leave a modest tip and tell the server you will write them a nice review.

- Souvenirs. Solution: fridge magnets only.

- Giving to the poor. (This one still gets me, but if you're giving away $10 a day - it adds up) Solution: volunteer your time instead and recognise that in tourist destinations many beggars are run by organised crime gangs.

Price v Comfort

I love traveling. I don't love struggling. I like decent accommodation, being able to eat properly and see places and enjoy. I am never in the mood for low-cost airlines or crappy transfers, so here's what I do to save money.

- Avoid organised tours unless you are going to a place where safety is a real issue. They are expensive and constrain your wanderlust to typical things. I only recommend them in Algeria, Iran and Papua New Guinea - where language and gender views pose serious problems all cured by a reputable tour organiser.

- Eat what the locals do.

- Cook in your Airbnb/ hostel where restaurants are expensive.

- Shop at local markets.

- Spend time choosing your flight, and check the operator on arilineratings.com

- Mix up hostels and Airbnbs. Hostels for meeting people, Airbnb for relaxing and feeling 'at home'.

Eat Hot Meals While You're Exploring

This is one hack that saves my family thousands a year. Using a thermos allows you to eat hot food while enjoying the sights. Here's a guide on how to do it effectively along with some recipes:

- **Choose the Right Thermos**: Look for thermoses with double-wall insulation and a wide mouth for easy filling and cleaning.
- **Preheat the Thermos**: Fill the thermos with boiling water and let it sit for a few minutes before pouring out the water and adding your hot food. This will help to maintain the temperature of your meal for longer.
- **Choose the right food**: soups, stews, pasta dishes, or even oatmeal for breakfast. Anything crispy will go soggy in the thermos.

Now, here are some food ideas that work well for packing in a thermos:

- **Hotdogs:** Just cook the dogs, pack buns and ketchup etc and you have a meal for four or more. This is great at outdoor markets with kids and can save you $20 + a day.
- **Chicken Congee**: A chicken porridge.
- **Vegetable Soup**: A hearty vegetable soup with beans or lentils is a satisfying and nutritious option. Make a big batch at home and portion it into the thermos for a warm and comforting meal on the go.
- **Chili**: Cook up a batch of your favorite chili recipe and pack it in the thermos. It's flavorful, filling, and perfect for chilly days.
- **Pasta with Tomato Sauce**: Cook your favorite pasta and toss it with a rich tomato sauce. This dish reheats well and tastes delicious straight from the thermos.
- **Curry**: Prepare a flavorful curry with vegetables, tofu, chicken, or meat of your choice. Serve it with rice or naan bread for a complete meal.
- **Oatmeal**: For breakfast on the go, make a batch of oatmeal with your favorite toppings such as nuts, fruits, and honey. It will stay warm and keep you full until lunchtime.

Not knowing where free toilets are

Use Toilet Finder - https://play.google.com/store/apps/details?id=com.bto.toilet&hl=en

Your Airbnb is awful

Airbnb customer service is notoriously bad. Help yourself out. Try to sort things out with the host, but if you can't, take photos of everything e.g bed, bathroom, mess, doors, contact them within 24 hours. Tell them you had to leave and pay for new accommodation. Ask politely for a full refund including booking fees. With photographic evidence and your new accommodation receipt, they can't refuse.

The airline loses your bag

Go to the Luggage desk before leaving the airport and report the bag missing. Hopefully you've headed the advice to put an AirTag in your checked bag and you can show them where to find your bag. Most airlines will give you an overnight bag, ask where you're staying and return the bag to you within three days. It's extremely rare for Airlines to lose your bag due to technological innovation, but if that happens you should submit an insurance claim after the three days is up, including receipts for everything you had to buy in the interim.

Your travel companion lets you down

Whether it's a breakup or a friend cancelling, it sucks and can ramp up costs. The easiest solution to finding a new travel companion is to go to a well-reviewed hostel and find someone you want to travel with. You should spend at least three days getting to know this person before you suggest travelling together. Finding someone in person is always better than finding someone online, because you can get a better idea of whether you will have a smooth journey together. Travel can make or break friendships.

Culture shock

I had one of the strongest culture shocks while spending 6 months in Japan. It was overwhelming how much I had to prepare when I went outside of the door (googling words and sentences what to use, where to go, which station and train line to use, what is this food called in Japanese and how does its look etc.). I was so tired constantly but in the end I just let go and went with my extremely bad Japanese. If you feel culture shocked its because your brain is referencing your surroundings to what you know. Stop comparing, have Google translate downloaded and relax.

Your Car rental insurance is crazy expensive

I always use carrentals.com and book with a credit card. Most credit cards will give you free insurance for the car, so you don't need to pay the extra. Some unsavoury companies will bump the price up when you arrive. Ask to speak to a manager. If this doesn't resolve, it google "consumer ombudsman for NAME OF COUNTRY." and seek an immediate full refund on the balance difference you paid. It is illegal in most countries to alter the price of a rental car when the person arrives to pickup a pre-arranged car.

A note on Car Rental Insurance

Always always always rent a car with a credit card that has rental vehicle coverage built into the card and is automatically applied when you rent a car. Then there's no need to buy additional rental insurance (check with your card on the coverage they protect some exclude collision coverage). Do yourself a favour when you step up to the desk to rent the car tell the agent you're already covered and won't be buying anything today. They work on commission and you'll save time and your patience avoiding the upselling.

You're sick

First off ALWAYS, purchase travel insurance. Including emergency transport up to $500k even to back home, which is usually less than $10 additional. I use https://www.comparethemarket.com/travel-insurance/ to find the best days. If I am sick I normally check into a hotel with room service and ride it out.

Make a Medication Travel Kit

Take travel sized medications with you:

- Antidiarrheal medication (for example, bismuth sub-salicylate, loperamide)

- Medicine for pain or fever (such as acetaminophen, aspirin, or ibuprofen)

- Throat Lozenges

Save yourself from most travel related hassles

- Do not make jokes with immigration and customs staff. A misunderstanding can lead to HUGE fines.

- Book the most direct flight you can find nonstop if possible.

- Carry a US$50 bill for emergency cash. I have entered a country and all ATM and credit card systems were down. US$ can be exchanged nearly anywhere in the world and is useful in extreme situations, but where possible don't exchange, as you will lose money.

- Check, and recheck, required visas and such BEFORE the day of your trip. Some countries, for instance, require a ticket out of the country in order to enter. Others, like the US and Australia, require electronic authorisation in advance.

- Airport security is asinine and inconsistent around the world. Keep this in mind when connecting flights. Always leave at least 2 hours for international connections or international to domestic. In Stansted for example, they force you to buy one of their plastic bags, and remove your liquids from your own plastic bag…. just to make money from you. And this adds to the time it will take to get through security, so lines are long.

- Wiki travel is perfect to use for a lay of the land.

- Expensive luggage rarely lasts longer than cheap luggage, in my experience. Fancy leather bags are toast with air travel.

Food

- When it comes to food, eat in local restaurants, not tourist-geared joints. Any place with the menu in three or more languages is going to be overpriced.

- Take a spork - a knife, spoon and fork all in one.

Water Bottle

Take a water bottle with a filter. We love these ones from Water to Go.

Empty it before airport security and separate the bottle and filter as some airport people will try and claim it has liquids…

Bug Sprays

If you're heading somewhere tropical spray your clothes with Permethrin before you travel. It lasts 40 washes and saves space in your bag. A 'Bite Away' zapper can be used after the bite to totally erase it. It cuts down on the itching and erases the bite from your skin.

Order free mini's

Don't buy those expensive travel sized toiletries, order travel sized freebies online. This gives you the opportunity to try brands you've never used before, and who knows, you might even find your new favourite soap.

Take a waterproof bag

If you're travelling alone you can swim without worrying about your phone, wallet and passport laying on the beach.

You can also use it as a source of entertainment on those ultra budget flights.

Make a private entertainment centre anywhere

Always take an eye-mask, earplugs, a scarf and a kindle reader - so you can sleep and entertain yourself anywhere!

The best Travel Gadgets

The door alarm

If you're nervous and staying in private rooms or airbnbs take a door alarm. For those times when you just don't feel safe, it can help you fall asleep. You can get tiny ones for less than $10 from Online Retailers: https://www.Online Retailers.com/Travel-door-alarm/s?k=Travel+door+alarm

Smart Blanket

Online Retailers sells a 6 in 1 heating blanket that is very useful for cold plane or bus trips. Its great if you have poor circulation as it becomes a detachable Foot Warmer: Online Retailers http://amzn.to/2hTYlOP I paid $49.00.

The coat that becomes a tent

https://www.adiff.com/products/tent-jacket. This is great if you're going to be doing a lot of camping.

Clever Tank Top with Secret Pockets

Keep your valuables safe in this top. Perfect for all climates. https://www.Online Retailers.com/Clever-Travel-Companion-Unisex-secret/dp/B00O94PXLE on Online Retailers for $39.90

Optical Camera Lens for Smartphones and Tablets

Leave your bulky camera at home. Turn your device into a high-performance camera. Buy on Online Retailers for $9.95

Travel-sized Wireless Router with USB Media Storage

Convert any wired network to a wireless network. Buy on Online Retailers for $17.99

Buy a Scrubba Bag to wash your clothes on the go

Or a cheaper imitable. You can wash your clothes on the go.

Hacks for Families

Rent an Airbnb apartment so you can cook

Apartments are much better for families, as you have all the amenities you'd have at home. They are normally cheaper per person too. We are the first travel guide publisher to include Airbnb's in our recommendations if you think any of these need updating you can email me at philgtang@gmail.com

Shop at local markets

Eat seasonal products and local products. Get closer to the local market and observe the prices and the offer. What you can find more easily, will be the cheapest.

Take Free Tours

Download free podcast tours of the destination you are visiting. The podcast will tell you where to start, where to go, and what to look for. Often you can find multiple podcast tours of the same place. Listen to all of them if you like, each one will tell you a little something new.

Pack Extra Ear Phones

If you go on a museum tour, they often have audio guides. Instead of having to rent one for each person, take some extra earphones. Most audio tour devices have a place to plug in a second set.

Buy Souvenirs Ahead of Time

If you are buying souvenirs somewhere touristy, you are paying a premium price. By ordering the same exact products online, you can save a lot of money.

Use Cheap Transportation

Do as the locals do, including weekly passes.

Carry Reusable Water Bottles

Spending money on water and other beverages can quickly add up. Instead of paying for drinks, take some refillable water bottles.

Combine Attractions

Many major cities offer ticket bundles where one price gets you into 5 or 6 popular attractions. You will need to plan ahead of time to decide what things you plan to do on vacation and see if they are selling these activities together.

Pack Snacks

Granola bars, apples, baby carrots, bananas, cheese crackers, juice boxes, pretzels, fruit snacks, apple sauce, grapes, and veggie chips.

Stick to Carry-On Bags

Do not pay to check a large bag. Even a small child can pull a carry-on.

Visit free art galleries and museums

Just google the name + free days.

Eat Street Food

There's a lot of unnecessary fear around this. You can watch the food prepared. Go for the stands that have a steady queue.

Travel Gadgets for Families

Dropcam

Are what-if scenarios playing out in your head? Then you need Dropcam.

'Dropcam HD Internet Wi-Fi Video Monitoring Cameras help you watch what you love from anywhere. In less than a minute, you'll have it setup and securely streaming video to you over your home Wi-Fi. Watch what you love while away with Dropcam HD.'

Approximate Price: $139

Kelty-Child-Carrier

Voted as one of the best hiking essentials if you're traveling with kids and can carry a child up to 18kg.

Jetkids Bedbox

No more giving up your own personal space on the plane with this suitcase that becomes a bed.

How to Believe Something You Don't Believe

"Our deepest fear is not that we are inadequate. Our deepest fear is that we are powerful beyond measure." Marianne Williamson.

To embark on a luxurious trip to New York on a budget requires more than just the tips in this book and financial planning; it demands a shift in mindset. It require you believing in abundance, in your ability to have anything you really want. While it may seem daunting, especially when faced with harsh realities of the cost of living crisis, etc, **fostering a belief in abundance is truly life-changing.**

The common advice is to "act as if" or "feel as if." I wholeheartedly concur, yet the challenge arises when one's circumstances appear far from prosperous. You're juggling multiple jobs, drowning in debt, and attempting to conjure the feeling of opulence? How is this even possible?

I understand this struggle intimately. I grew up poor in London. I was a kid from a run-down council estate where gang violence sent nine of my closest friends to prison. I went to an average state school. At 19 I went to one of England's elite universities to study Law. Out of 2,000 students, it was just me who didn't come from a background of privilege. Talk about a fish out of water?

I didn't just feel poor; I was. My clothes had holes, I couldn't afford a laptop or even books (even on a scholarship) and don't even get me started on culture and etiquette. It felt like I was playing a game without knowing the rules. I was about to quit and then my dad said this : "You are better than everyone here because you earned you spot. You've weathered losses that would break others." It was a lie, a big fat one, that would hurt me later, but boy, did it get me through law school.

I graduated top of my class, secured a prestigious job, and even launched my own successful business. Yet, despite my newfound wealth and the errant belief that I was "better", I still felt like the kid from the council estate with holes in my shoes.

Life gives you what you believe. I lost most of my money investing in a start-up, and of course, I found a strange comfort in my familiar poverty. **This sparked an introspective journey: How could I believe in abundance and success when my own mind seemed to be comfortable in poverty? How could I believe something I didn't believe?**

First, I recognized that abundance comes in many forms. I replaced 'money' with 'abundance.' Somehow, this just felt way less stressful than the word 'money.' I don't know how it feels for you, but try it out.

I was pretty horrified to release my core belief was I was somehow better off poor but when I finally did, I embarked on the journey to transform my relationship with abundance. Since undertaking this journey in 2016. I've accomplished significant milestones: purchasing a home in Vienna, pursuing my passion for writing travel guides, getting married, having two children, and embracing abundance. **These are the exact steps I took to believe...**

Affirmations

Affirmations are positive statements that challenge self-sabotaging and negative thoughts. Repeating these affirmations make most people feel like "this is a load of bull". That's why you have to find a belief that is believable and specific to the desired outcome you are going for. Was it true that I was better than everyone at the University because I came from poverty? No. It most definitely wasn't, but believing it gave me the confidence I needed to succeed (and fuelled my ego).

- **Find your believable affirmation**: You could start with "I'm in the process of taking lots of luxury vacations every year". If you add "I'm in the process" it makes it way more believable. In the beginning, I just repeated to myself: 'I can have everything and anything I desire.'
- **Consistency in Writing:** It's crucial to write down affirmations daily, preferably in the morning and before bed, to strengthen the new belief. Merely placing them somewhere isn't enough; research suggests that when we're constantly exposed to something, we tune it out. By physically writing out the affirmations, you engage muscle memory, imprinting them more deeply.

Visualization

Used widely in sports psychology and personal development for its effectiveness in enhancing performance and fostering belief in one's abilities. "If you go there in the mind, you're go there in the body."

- **Detailed Imagery:** The more detailed your visualization, the more effective it will be. Imagine the sights, sounds, and feelings associated with your desired belief or outcome. You might imagine, the hot sun on your back, the air skirting over your skin in that air-con'ed bar.

- **Know it works**: A study published in Psychosomatic Medicine investigated the effects of pre-surgery visualization on surgical outcomes. Patients who practiced guided imagery and visualization before undergoing surgery experienced shorter hospital stays, fewer postoperative complications, and faster recovery times compared to those who didn't engage in visualization exercises. This research shows that mental rehearsal can positively impact surgical outcomes and recovery processes. If it can affect surgery outcomes, it can affect your vacation!

- **Visualise your rich person problems**: My first job out of university was risk assessment. I was promoted again and again because I could identify the risks of any endeavor within 15 seconds. My brain still works like that. I take my 3-year-old swimming, and before we've even gotten in the pool, I've identified 14 threats and a flat surface to deliver CPR to her... It's a human trait to worry so why not use your ability to worry to your advantage? Imagine all the "problems" you'll have when you're abundant. Your cocktail on a tropical beach might be too cold. You might forget to tax-deduct all the donations you made to charities. You might tip someone really well and find them hugging you desperately. Don't take this too far; you don't want to manifest actual problems, but it definitely redirects your mind to believe you are rich.

Mo' Money Mo' Problems isn't true

Contrary to the popular notion that "more money, more problems," recent studies suggest otherwise. Achieving a certain level of financial comfort alleviates many concerns. Research indicates that individuals who feel financially secure tend to experience higher levels of overall life satisfaction and lower levels of stress. This comfort allows for greater flexibility in decision-making, reduces anxiety about meeting basic needs, and provides a sense of stability for the future. While excessive wealth does not necessarily equate to happiness, having enough resources to cover necessities and pursue meaningful experiences significantly enhance your quality of life.

Behavioral Experiments

Behavioral experiments involve acting as if you already hold the new belief. This "fake it till you make it" approach can gradually shift your internal beliefs to align with your actions.

- **Dress the Part:** In London we say "If you look good, you feel good." Consider upgrading your look. This doesn't mean splurging on designer brands; it's about being smart and feeling good in what you wear. Think of it as costume design for the movie of your life where you're the wealthy protagonist. Clean, well-fitted, and confident clothes can change your self-perception and how others perceive you.
- **Focus on Abundance:** Redirect your attention towards abundance rather than scarcity. Instead of dwelling on what you lack, consciously focus on the abundance that surrounds you, such as the beauty of nature, the support of loved ones, or the opportunities to travel. When you see a beautiful car, say to yourself, someone else has that beautiful car, I can have one too, thanks for showing me, it's possible.
- **Create an Abundance Journal:** Keep a journal dedicated to recording moments of abundance, gratitude, and success in your life. Regularly write down your achievements, blessings, and things you're thankful for.

- **Steal beliefs**: Once my friend who is never sick said, "No bacteria could ever conquer me," I decided to adopt the same mindset and my stomach issues, especially while traveling in India, disappeared. If you hear someone say "money always comes so easy to me" don't be jealous, just start affirming that for yourself.
- **Help people:** When we give to others of compliments, time, praise, money, it is always returned to us and can let our minds know, we have enough to share.
- **Spend a day being aware of your thoughts:** Identify and challenge any limiting beliefs you have about money, such as "money is hard to come by" or "I'll never be wealthy." Replace these beliefs with thoughts, such as "I am capable of creating wealth" or "I attract abundance into my life effortlessly." The prefrontal cortex produces our thoughts. It is 40% of our entire brain. This region, located at the front of the brain is not producing stone cold facts. It's pulling information from life experience and things around us to generate thoughts.

Trying to believe something you don't yet believe is about making a genuine effort to adopt a new belief, and it feels very challenging at first. Dismissing the importance of financial abundance overlooks the practical realities of navigating the world we live in and the opportunities it presents. Set your intention to believe it is right for you to be abundant and keep looking for evidence that it is true - and gradually you will believe you are entitled to all the abundance life has to offer. You do!

How I got hooked on luxury on a budget travelling

"We're on holiday" is what my dad used to say, justifying our accumulation of debt that eventually led to losing our home and possessions when I was 11. We transitioned from the suburban tranquility of Hemel Hempstead to a dilapidated council estate in inner-city London, near my dad's new job as a refuge collector, a euphemism for a dustbin man. I watched my dad go through a nervous breakdown while losing touch with all my school friends.

My dad reveled in striding up to hotel lobby desks without a care, repeatedly booking overpriced holidays on credit cards. The reality hit hard—we couldn't afford any of them. Eventually, my dad had no option but to declare bankruptcy. When my mum discovered the extent of our debt, our family unit disintegrated—a succinct, albeit painful, summary of events that steered me towards my life's passion: budget travel without compromising on enjoyment, safety, or comfort.

At 22, I embarked on full-time travel, writing the inaugural Super Cheap Insider guide for friends visiting Norway, a venture I accomplished on less than $250 over a month.. I understand firsthand the suffocating burden of debt and how the flippant notion of "we're on vacation" fails to absolve financial responsibility; in fact, it contradicts the essence of travel—freedom.

Many skeptics deemed my dream of LUXURY budget travel unattainable. I hope this guide proves otherwise, showcasing insider hacks that render budget travel luxurious.

And if my tale of hardship brought you down, I apologize. My dad has since remarried and happily works as a chef at a prestigious hotel in London—the kind he used to take us to!

A final word...

There's a simple system you can use to think about budget travel. In life, we can choose two of the following: cheap, fast, or quality. So if you want it cheap and fast, you will get lower quality service. Fast-food is the perfect example. The system holds true for purchasing anything while traveling. I always choose cheap and quality, except at times when I am really limited on time. Normally, you can make small tweaks to make this work for you. Ultimately, you must make choices about what's most important to you and heed your heart's desires.

'Your heart is the most powerful muscle in your body. Do what it says.' Jen Sincero

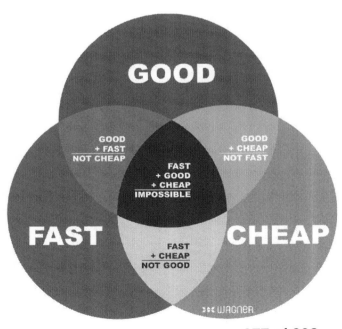

If you've found this book useful, please select five stars, it would mean genuinely make my day to see I've helped you.

Copyright

Made in the USA
Middletown, DE
10 November 2024

64237835R00157